Jump Back in Time

Jump Back in Time

A Living History Resource

Written and illustrated by
Carol Peterson

TEACHER IDEAS PRESS
Portsmouth, NH

Teacher Ideas Press
A division of Reed Elsevier Inc.
361 Hanover Street
Portsmouth, NH 03801–3912
www.teacherideaspress.com

Offices and agents throughout the world

Library of Congress Cataloging-in-Publication Data

Peterson, Carol

    Jump back in time : a living history resource / written and illustrated by Carol Peterson.
      p. cm.
    Includes bibliographical references.
    ISBN 1-59158-067-6
    1. History—Study and teaching (Elementary)—Activity programs—United States. 2. United
    States—History—Study and teaching (Elementary)—Activity programs. I. Title.
  LB1582.U6 P48 2003
  372.89—dc21   2003014844

Editor: Suzanne Barchers
Production Coordinator: Angela Laughlin
Typesetter: Westchester Book Services
Cover design: Gaile Ivaska
Manufacturing: Steve Bernier

Printed in the United States of America on acid-free paper

08 07 06 05 04 ML 1 2 3 4 5

This book is dedicated to all the people who have and will make up the history of this world, but especially to Jim, Doug, and Nicole who have filled my personal history with joy.

Contents

Jump Back in Time

Chapter 1

Bringing History to Life

Imagine tapping out Morse coded messages, flicking beads on an abacus, and practicing hunting skills, while the aroma of tortillas fills the air. Kids don't want to hear about history—they want to live it!

A living history event makes history fun. Hands-on activities, games, and food make an ideal end-of-year school celebration or can fire up kids for a social studies unit to come. With opportunities for costumes and take home "goodies," a living history event is also a unique educational, nonfrightening Halloween alternative for school, scouting, and charity fund-raisers. Whatever the setting, when kids experience the culture and daily activities of people in history, they gain understanding they can't find in textbooks.

HOW TO USE THIS RESOURCE

This resource contains instructions for presenting four living history events, each consisting of a full day of activities. These events, which can be coordinated with school social studies curriculum standards, scouting awards, or just for the fun of it, are:

1. Ancient Cultures Day—a glimpse at selected ancient cultures

2. Native American Culture Day—a sampling of Native American groups based on geographical regions

3. Colonial America Day—a sneak peek at life in the 13 colonies

4. Pioneer Day—a taste of American westward expansion

Everything to plan a living history event is here—instructions, recipes, checklists, and tips to vary each activity. An appendix provides scheduling charts to get organized and sample notes to help you communicate with parents and volunteers. Also included are reproducible handouts so kids can create souvenir booklets that will keep them learning after the day is over. Many of these handout pages can themselves be expanded into additional activities.

A typical living history event is presented as a full day of activities. Groups of children rotate through 10–15 stations with one adult supervisor per station. Stations are organized by theme. Pioneer Day themes, for example, include the journey west, Chinese culture in the west, Spanish culture in the west, Native American culture in the west, railroads and telegraphs, and pioneer life. Choose one or more stations from each theme but include all themes for a well-rounded event.

STRUCTURING YOUR LIVING HISTORY EVENT

Here are some things to keep in mind when planning your living history event:

1. Children rotate through stations in groups of 8–12. You will need the same number of groups as the number of mid-day stations you have chosen, so that all stations are being used throughout the day. Designate which children will be in each group ahead of time to avoid squabbles and delay. All children in a group will have the same kid-friendly group name. Color-coded group nametags (red for "Pyramid Builders"; blue for "Hammurabi's Heroes," for example) aid in quick identification. An even number of children per group works best for station activities requiring pairs.

2. Keep children in their original groups and maintain their rotation order throughout the day. For example, to reduce confusion and maintain traffic flow, the same "Buffalo Hunters" will follow the same "Tumbleweeds" through all rotations until everyone reassembles at the end of the day.

3. To assist with organization and instruction, start the day with an activity at station 1 that all children participate in together. Then begin the rotation, starting one group of children at station 2, one group at station 3, and so forth. At the next rotation, all children at station 2 will move to station 3; all children at station 3 will move to station 4; all children at the last station will move to station 2.

4. Use the Sample Rotation Schedule (Appendix 1) as a guide to plan your day. Allow 30 minutes for each beginning and end-of-day activity, 15–20 minutes for each mid-day station, and 3–5 minutes for each rotation.

5. Schedule like-themed activities one after the other so kids finish one theme before moving to the next. For example, during Native American Culture Day, kids should participate in all Plains activities before rotating to the Southwestern stations.

6. Designate one person in charge of timing. Use a bell, drum, bullhorn, or other noisemaker to signal station rotations. Rely heavily on a stopwatch or kitchen timer. Keep groups moving but have recess or specifically scheduled bathroom breaks throughout the day.

7. Provide each child with a bag to collect crafts and handouts. One suggested start-of-day activity is to make a gathering bag. A simple gathering bag can be made from a sheet of heavy paper (18" × 24" or larger) folded in half, stapled at the sides, and decorated with crayons or markers. Make sure each child puts his or her name on the gathering bag. There are suggested activities, such as singing and storytelling, for children to do while preparing their gathering bags. Alternatively, gathering bags can be made ahead of time as a previous school or scouting project, and, of course, plastic or paper grocery bags work in a pinch.

8. Children receive printed handouts at each station to create a souvenir booklet. Booklets are assembled at one of the final stations, generally along with group photos or an end-of-day feast. Provide two sheets of 8½" × 11" paper per child, slip handouts inside, and staple. Children can decorate the cover with colored markers or crayons while participating in discussions about what they learned and how life is different today. Make sure to have a camera and extra film handy at this station and throughout the day.

9. Teachers may want to keep grade-level curriculum standards in mind when choosing which event to present. Schools can present school-wide events over several years to cover multiple curriculum standards. Scouting groups can select events to coincide with badges and award requirements.

10. Don't forget local resources when planning your event. Relatives, museum docents, historians, craftsmen, and artists love to share their knowledge or culture with kids. People will be more willing to volunteer an hour or two than a whole day though, so try to schedule their participation at the beginning or end of the day when they can give their presentation once to the whole group.

11. Pool resources with other leaders. Teachers, for example, can cooperate with same-grade teachers in their school or community for a single living history event. Similarly, fourth grade teachers presenting an end-of-the year Pioneer Day might consider including graduating third graders and their teachers and parent volunteers.

12. Reproducible scheduling aids and notices are provided to help you plan your event. Use Appendix 1, the Sample Rotation Schedule, as a guide to help schedule your rotations. Use Appendix 2, the Master Volunteer Schedule, to help coordinate volunteers. Appendixes 3, 4, and 5 can be used to communicate with parents, volunteers, and people who may be donating supplies for your event.

HOW TO RESIZE AN EVENT

What if you can't set aside a whole day for living history? What if you are low on volunteers? What if you want to present living history to a smaller group of children? Or a larger one?

Jump Back in Time living history events are ideally suited for a large number of children—three classrooms, or a Cub Scout pack, for example. But because of their flexibility, they can just as easily be presented in other formats. For example, if time and volunteers are limited, teachers can present a living history "week" by scheduling one or more activities per day. Similarly, scout leaders can present a living history "month" by scheduling a few activities per meeting over several weeks. To schedule a Pioneer Week, you might present a Westward Ho! mini event on Monday, a Home on the Range mini event on Tuesday, and so on.

If you are presenting an event for fewer children, you can either make your groups smaller—5–6 children each—or you can have two or three larger groups of 10–15 children each. Although it is easier to maintain control within smaller groups, a fewer number of large groups means that not all stations need to be presented at the same time. Four larger groups, for example, could rotate in the morning through one combined station followed by four rotations and then through four rotations followed by one combined station in the afternoon, thus reducing the number of adult leaders needed. You should, however, allow an additional 5 minutes per station for larger groups, which tend to waste more time in disorganization.

If you are planning a larger event—a schoolwide affair or fund-raiser, for example—you will want to structure it so that each child's participation is approximately one to two hours. Therefore you will choose 4–6 rotation stations. Children can participate in the beginning activities while they are waiting to start the rotation. Consistent and firm rotation timing is even more important at larger events to maintain organization and traffic flow. Additionally, for these larger events, remember to specify a firm time when the last group of children begins the rotation process so that you can ultimately end the event.

TIPS FOR EXTRA FUN

Each activity in this manual can be completed within a 15–20 minute period. It is generally better to keep kids moving than for them to have time left over with nothing to do. Therefore, this resource includes "Tips for Extra Fun" for each station with ideas for additional activities or enhancements that can be done at that station. Here are some tips to make the whole event more fun.

- Be sure to renumber your stations, if needed. For example, if you plan a Colonial America Day using only 10 of the possible 16 stations, renumber yours 1–10.

- Whenever possible, precut paper patterns and string and pre-punch holes to help the day move more smoothly.

- Provide small prizes, candies, ribbons, or classroom points for game winners.

- Signs with the station name and number at each station help direct traffic. Large computer-printed banners are great, but simple handwritten signs are just as effective. Whenever possible, personalize stations with adult leader, town, and school names. For example, stations named "Mission del Smith," "Mrs. Gregory's Better Butter Shop," and "Brookville Railroad" make the day more fun.

- When scheduling rotations, try alternating indoor and outdoor activities, crafts and games, standing and sitting.

- Consider having water or punch (and cups) at some stations and have access to soap and water, hand sanitizer, or wipes when cooking and eating.

- A shaded rule at the top and bottom of pages in this book indicates patterns, maps, handouts, or stories intended to be photocopied and used for your event. In addition, you may wish to make single copies of station instructions and text meant to be read aloud. Note that maps are to be used as reference and are not intended to be precise in detail.

- Encourage kids and leaders to dress in costume. Many diverse peoples lived throughout history, so ethnic costumes of all kinds work for these events. Ideas for simple costumes, props, and accessories are included at the beginning of each unit. A red bandana or a Grecian sheet "toga" may be all that's needed to get kids in the mood. At least consider providing a few costumes or props for end-of-day group photographs.

- Let local media and businesses know what you're doing. A bit of publicity and community awareness often yields volunteers and donated supplies. It might even help you snag a local historian or celebrity to spin tales for your start or end of day.

NOW JUMP BACK IN TIME!

Based on the guidelines in this manual, Pioneer Day was presented to groups of 100 fourth graders three separate years at a California public school, despite strict fingerprinting requirements that limited the number of volunteers available. You can do it, too.

Whether you want a single day of fun or a week of mini events. Whether you want to present living history to 20 kids or 1,000. Whatever part of the world and place in history you want to share with children—you can do it. Simply don your toga, slip into your moccasins, grab your quill pen, and start planning. Can't you almost smell those tortillas sizzling on the griddle? Don't just imagine history. Grab those kids, jump back in time, and live it!

Chapter 2

Ancient Cultures Day

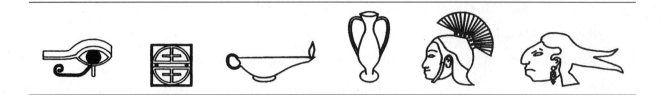

Welcome to Ancient Cultures Day. During this day of fun, children will rotate through stations sampling the ancient cultures of the Near East, Egypt, China, Greece, Rome, and Mesoamerica. They will start the day as a single group, participating in organizational activities to gear them up for learning. Then they will split into smaller groups, rotate through stations, and join up again at the end of the day with activities to summarize what they've learned. If you choose not to include the first station from each culture, still plan to include a discussion and coloring of the map and timeline. The stations and activities for Ancient Cultures Day are:

Start the Day as a Group

Station 1. Enter the Time Machine (Pin the Culture on the Map, Timeline, gathering bag, and myths. Children split into groups and proceed to remaining stations.)

Welcome to the Ancient Near East

Station 2. Muddy Math (Map, Timeline, Cuneiform Clay Activity)

Station 3. King David's Music Shop (Make Lyres)

Welcome to Ancient Egypt

Station 4. Royal Cartouche Shop (Map, Timeline, Name in Hieroglyphics)

Station 5. King Tut's House of Games (Oware Game)

Welcome to Ancient China

Station 6. Emperor Qin's Army (Map, Timeline, Clay Figures)

Station 7. Calligraphy Card Shop (Calligraphy Scrolls)

Welcome to Ancient Greece

Station 8. Greek Sandal Shop (Map, Timeline, Sandals)

Station 9. Alexander's Great Library (Write Name in Greek)

Welcome to Ancient Rome

Station 10. Julian Calendar (Map, Timeline, Calendar with Roman Months)

Station 11. Mosaic Masterpieces (Group Mosaic, Roman Numerals)

Welcome to Ancient Mesoamerica

Station 12. Chocolate Checkers (Map, Timeline, Bul Board Game)

Station 13. Pok-A-Tok (Ball Game, Myth)

End the Day as a Group

Station 14. Atop Mt. Olympus (Olympic Games)

Station 15. Make-Your-Own Rosetta Stone

Station 16. Ancient Snack Shack (Snacks, Group Photos, Souvenir Booklet)

NAMETAGS

Use the following for group nametags or think up some of your own:

Hammurabi's Heroes	Mayans	Minoans
Pyramid Builders	Ball Players	Friends and Romans
Pharaohs	Babylonians	Caesar's Citizens
Mummy Makers	Sumerians	Dynasty Builders
Aztecs	Olympians	Qin's Army

COSTUME IDEAS

Ancient people didn't have sewing machines, so clothing was simple—usually a piece of cloth tied or pinned around the body. Use sheets, tablecloths, light blankets, thin towels, and fabric remnants for simple clothing, worn over street clothes, making sure the costume is short enough to avoid tripping over the hem. Cut and staple ends of lightweight cardboard or heavy paper and cover in foil for bracelets, headbands, and other jewelry.

Near East: Tunics—long unfitted dresses that came to the knees (for boys) and ankles (for boys and girls). Loose, pullover adult shirts make kid-sized tunics. Cloaks were large cloths draped over tunics. Girls wore cloaks over their heads; boys wrapped them around their shoulders. Props and accessories: long stick to carry as a staff, scrolls of rolled paper.

Egypt: Short tunics and kilts. A narrow cloth can be tied around the waist to hang just above the knee. Props and accessories: jewelry—gold, deep blue, and orange colors were popular. Collars can be made from a brown paper bag or colored construction paper—cut into a semicircle with a slit at the back and decorated with bright colors and hieroglyphics.

China: Wrap-around bathrobes make simple Chinese robes; solid pants cut mid calf and a plain colored shirt make simple peasant clothes. Props and accessories: umbrellas; green paper jewelry simulates jade; decorate a sheet of paper, crease like an accordion, fold in half, and tape the bottom for a paper fan.

Greece: A chiton (KI-ton) was a large piece of cloth wrapped around the body and pinned at the shoulder. Boys wore theirs to the knee; girls wore them to the ankle and tied at the waist or hips. Props and accessories: jewelry—necklaces and bracelets, laurel wreaths (plastic vines tied around the head).

Rome: Boys wore a knee-length tunic with short sleeves and a belt. A toga (a long sheet of cloth) was worn over the tunic—wrapped around the body, underneath the right arm, and draped over the left shoulder. Girls wore a long tunic with a short tunic called a "stola" over it. When girls went outside, they draped a cloak "palla" over them. Props and accessories: sandals, cardboard shields covered in aluminum foil. For bracelets, cut cardboard or heavy paper, staple ends, and wrap in foil. Scrolls. Comedy and tragedy masks used by actors: cut "eyes" and "mouth" out of paper plates; punch holes on each side, attach string, and decorate. Laurel wreaths (see Greek costume description above).

Mesoamerica: Loincloths for boys with decorated flaps front and back. Make loincloths from brown paper bags cut open—decorate with felt pens, fold down the top, and punch holes at each top corner. Tie together with string and wear over clothes. Girls: wrap-around skirts and tuniclike blouses. Boys and girls wore capes—a length of fabric tied at one shoulder. Props and accessories: face paint and knee ornaments (aluminum covered cardboard bands) for boys, colorful beaded necklaces for boys and girls, hair ribbons for girls, feathers; flutes, rattles, balls.

START THE DAY AS A GROUP

Station 1. Enter the Time Machine

All children are assembled at this station, placed into rotation groups, and given nametags and instructions. Read some or all of the myths while children are making their gathering bags (see Chapter 1). Suggest they decorate their gathering bags with scenes from myths, map locations, or something else that represents one of the cultures. Then, using the *Jump Back* World Map of Ancient Cultures as a guide, play Pin the Culture on the Map. Children take turns marking the location of ancient cultures that will be presented during the day on a large map with sticky notes. Distribute copies of the Timeline to the children. Children will highlight relevant sections throughout the day. For this station you will need:

- These instructions
- Ancient myths
- A large world map
- *Jump Back* World Map of Ancient Cultures (copy for each child)
- Sticky notes—1 each for Near East, Egypt, China, Greece, Rome, Mesoamerica
- *Jump Back* Timeline (copy for each child)
- Items to make gathering bags (see Chapter 1)

TIPS FOR EXTRA FUN

- Background music adds fun. Try the public library for music from countries being studied. Although the music will be contemporary, it will help get kids in the mood.
- Ask children dressed in costume to explain what culture they represent.
- Provide costumes or accessories for kids to try on or wear throughout the day—beads, togas, etc., or provide costumes at the first station of each culture to wear only at that station.

Ancient Myths

Background notes at the end of these myths can be read aloud or used for further discussion. Myths from different cultures were often similar. Many cultures, for example, believed in one main god and several less important gods who controlled specific parts of nature. Sometimes the gods were seen as cruel and stories were often violent and bloody. Myths are grouped by topic:

Sun God myths: "The Tenth Son" (Chinese) and "Bloodthirsty Gods" (Egyptian)

Weather God myths: "Dragon Feast" (Hittite) and "The Four Musicians" (Mayan)

City myths: "The Best Gift" (Greek) and "Brothers Who Didn't Share" (Roman)

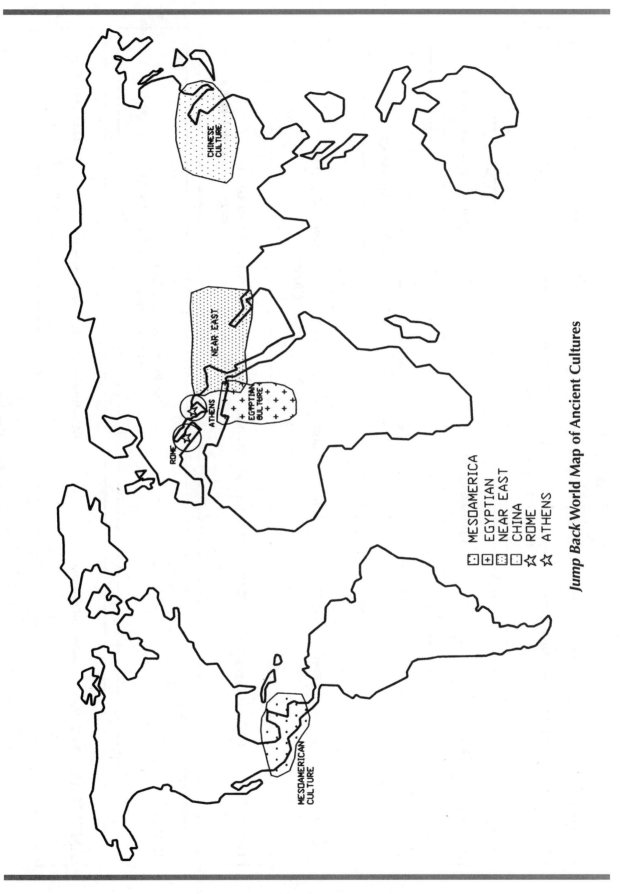

Jump Back World Map of Ancient Cultures

⊡ MESOAMERICA
⊞ EGYPTIAN
⊡ NEAR EAST
⊡ CHINA
☆ ROME
☆ ATHENS

TIMELINE

NEAR EAST 3100 BC -- Sumerian/Assyrian/Babylonians   1350 Moses   625 BC Fall of Babylon
1700 BC Hammurabi   1100-722 BC Kingdom of Israel

EGYPT 3100 BC --   Egyptian Empire   --   31 AD Egypt under Roman control

CHINA 2200 BC -- Chinese Dynasties -- 500 BC (Buddha)
214 BC Great Wall (Emperor Qin)

BC   **AD**
3500 -- 3000 -- 2500 -- 2000 -- 1500 -- 1000 -- 500 -- 0 -- 500 -- 1000 -- 1500

Birth of
Jesus Christ

GREECE 3000BC -- Minoans -- 2000 BC   1600-1200 BC Mycenae   336-323 BC Alexander the Great
500BC -- 200 AD Golden -- Hellenistic Greek ages

ROME   753 BC Founding of Rome
510 BC -- Roman Empire -- 476 AD

AMERICAS 3372 BC date on Mayan calendar   1100-400 BC Olmecs   200 BC-900AD Mayan   1440-1521 Aztec
900-1200 AD Toltec

Jump Back Timeline

The Tenth Son (Chinese)

Di Jun, god of the eastern sky and his wife, Xi He, were blessed with ten strong, bright sons. Xi He dressed her sons in golden pants, orange shirts, and fiery red capes. Then every morning she harnessed a dragon to her chariot and drove one of the boys to the edge of the world. There she kissed him good-bye and left him to walk home across the sky.

The strong, bright boys of the god of the eastern sky were ten burning suns. Each son took his turn lighting the sky and warming the earth. As the sons grew older, however, they didn't want to wait ten days for their turn to shine and decided it would be more fun to make the long walk home together. So the naughty boys began to make the journey together each day—ten bright, hot suns in the sky.

But ten suns at once were too much for the world. The waters on the earth began to dry. The trees and crops burned until the earth was black. Humans no longer knew a moment of coolness; no shelter of darkness for sleep.

The Emperor traveled to Di Jun's house. "Please control your children!" pleaded the Emperor. "The world is dying!"

"Our sons will not obey us," sobbed Xi He. "But we will not let the people die." She sent for Yi, the archer.

With his magic bow and ten white arrows, Yi set off to shoot down the ten suns. Yi fired his white arrows. One. Two. Three. Three suns exploded and fell to the earth.

"Thank you, Xi He," cried the humans, watching Yi shoot. "For being willing to sacrifice your ten sons for us."

Oh, no! thought the Emperor. *If all ten sons are killed, the world will be left without heat and light. The earth will freeze. Humans will die.*

"Servant!" yelled the Emperor. "Find the archer and steal one of his white arrows before he kills all of the suns."

The servant ran after Yi and snatched the last arrow from him, just as the tenth sun ran terrified toward the horizon.

The next morning, the tenth sun was still afraid. "Don't make me walk the sky, mother!" he begged.

"Behave!" ordered his mother, bundling him into the chariot and sending him on his way.

And the tenth sun has behaved—ever since.

Background Notes: The ancient Chinese calendar had ten days in a week. The people believed there was a separate sun for each of the ten days. Very few ancient Chinese myths have survived because they were not often written down. Fortunately, this story was remembered and included as part of a "modern" poem written nearly 2,400 years ago.

Bloodthirsty Gods (Egyptian)

One day, when the world was new, the great sun god, Ra, wondered where his children, Shu (shoo), god of air, and Tefnut (TEF-nut), goddess of moisture, had gone.

"Shu! Tefnut!" he called. But his children didn't come. So Ra plucked the eye from his head (which—being a god—was an easy thing to do). His eye took the form of the sun and Ra threw it into the sky to search for his children. Since Ra needed an eye to keep track of the universe, he made himself a new eye until the old one returned.

When Ra's eye had found his children, it yelled at Ra. "Why have you replaced me?" The first eye scolded Ra until Ra wept.

Ra's tears splattered over the earth, becoming humans as they landed. Ra was delighted. He loved ruling over the humans. But Ra was sometimes crabby. One day, he decided humans were not worshiping him enough. Once more, he plucked out his eye. This time, it took the form of Hathor (HA-thor), the goddess of love and family.

"Punish the humans!" roared Ra, as he sent her to earth.

Usually Hathor was kind and gentle, but because Ra was angry, his eye, in the shape of Hathor, was angry, too, and she began to kill the humans. "I have tasted human blood," she shrieked, "and will drink every last drop!"

"Oh, no!" said Ra. "If I don't stop Hathor, there will be no humans left for me to rule!"

That night, his eye (since it was both the sun and Hathor) slept. Ra sent his servants to gather red earth from an island in the Nile River. "Mix this red earth with 7,000 jars of beer," he commanded. Then Ra ordered them to pour the beer out over the fields.

The next morning, Hathor awoke and saw the flood of red beer. "Human blood from those I killed yesterday!" she thought, still in a rage. Hathor began to drink the beer and soon finished all 7,000 jars!

Ra watched Hathor fall into a drunken sleep. Then he snatched back his eye. When the eye was sober, both Ra and Hathor once again gazed down at humans with kindness and love.

Background Notes: The ancient Egyptians believed the sun god, Ra, was immortal because he died every night (as the setting sun) and was reborn again every morning. Since Ra could remove his eye and send it about the universe, an eye is a symbol often used to represent him.

The Four Musicians (Mayan)

In the beginning of the world, there was no color and the only sounds on earth were the roaring of the waves, the moaning of men, and the crying of babies. Shadows flew away from the sun to hide on earth.

When the Lord of All Things saw this, he called to Lord of the Wind. "The world should be full of color and song," he said. "Go to the House of the Sun and take the four musicians to the world. But beware! The musicians' sweet music has still not made the Sun kind."

Lord of the Wind flew to the House of the Sun where the four musicians were playing songs and dancing. One, dressed in yellow, played a song of love on her flute. One, dressed in red, played a song of joy on his drum. One, dressed in blue, played a song of dreams on her shell. One, dressed in green, played a song of heaven on his bells.

When the Sun saw Lord of the Wind, he told the musicians, "Lord of the Wind has come to take you to earth. But the world is a dark and sad place, so hide from Lord of the Wind."

Lord of the Wind called to the musicians. "Musicians, the world needs your beauty, your color, and music. Come to me."

Again and again Lord of the Wind called to the musicians, but the Sun had made them afraid and they hid. So Lord of the Wind made lightning strike and thunder boom.

"The House of the Sun is being attacked!" cried the musicians as they ran from their hiding place. One by one, they leaped into Lord of the Wind's arms. "Save us!" they cried.

Lord of the Wind carried the musicians to earth, whispering, "Come where you are needed most."

The musicians saw the gray sadness and heard the silence on the earth. Bravely they began to play their songs. Lord of the Wind carried their color and music around the earth and soon the world was filled with happiness.

When the Sun saw the change in the world, his anger vanished. He shone his light down upon the world. The shadows on earth tried to hide from the Sun, but the Sun shone his light more brightly until once—each day—shadows fled completely in the noontime sun.

The Sun was happy. The world was happy. And the Lord of All Things was pleased.

Background Notes: Lord of the Wind is also known in Mesoamerican stories as Quetzalcoatl (quat-zal-COAT-al), a feathered snake that sometimes appeared as the planet Venus and as a light-skinned, bearded human who would return one day. When the Spanish invaded Mexico 3,000 years later, the Aztecs mistook the bearded Cortez for Quetzalcoatl and welcomed him as a god. Cortez and his men easily took Mexico from them.

May be copied for classroom use. *Jump Back in Time: A Living History Resource* by Carol Peterson
(Teacher Ideas Press, Portsmouth, NH), © 2004.

Dragon Feast (Hittite)

"A dragon!" everyone shouted. "Run!"

The storm god watched his people scatter over the earth as the terrifying dragon, Illuyankas (Il-oo-YAN-kus), destroyed cities and breathed fire over the land. The storm god armed himself for battle and called to Illuyankas.

"Illuyankas! Stop!" The storm god threw a lightning bolt at Illuyankas.

Illuyankas snapped at the lightning bolt and spat it out, turning the green hills to ashes.

"Illuyankas! Beware!" roared the storm god, hurling wind and rain against the dragon's rough hide.

Illuyankas raised his mighty head and the rain sizzled off his steaming scales.

The storm god heaved snowstorms and blizzards and hurricanes at the dragon, but each time, Illuyankas shook them off and breathed his fiery breath across the land. Then he flicked his tail, tossed the storm god back into the sky, and stomped his claws, cracking open the surface of the earth. Thousands of his dragon children squeezed up through the cracks, snarling, bellowing, and snorting flames.

"Welcome, splendid creatures," said a kindly voice behind Illuyankas. "Won't you enjoy this meal I have prepared for you?"

"Who are you?" bellowed Illuyankas, casting his red eyes on the lovely woman.

"I am Inaras (Ih-NAR-us), goddess of wild animals," she said sweetly. "You must be tired after fighting my father, the storm god. Rest and eat." She pointed to a feast laid out on the ground. Golden plates were filled with every kind of food—meat, fruit, cheese, and cakes—piled higher than hills.

The dragons sniffed at the food. The fire in their mouths sputtered in the drool that dripped from their hungry lips. For three days and nights the dragons ate as Inaras kept the plates full of her delicious food.

At last, sleepy and full, the dragons turned from Inaras' feast and trudged back to the cracks in the earth to return to their underground lair. They dove their great heads into the earth. They shoved their enormous necks under the ground. They wiggled their gigantic chests into the soil. But no matter how hard they dove and shoved and wiggled, their full bellies would not fit back through the cracks.

"Come, Father," sang Inaras. "The dragons' fierce heads are trapped."

The storm god returned with the other gods. The people ran from their hiding places. Together the gods and the people killed the dragons.

"Thank you, Inaras!" the people cheered. "Thank you, storm god!"

The people rejoiced. And the storm god, seeing the destruction caused by Illuyankas, withheld bad weather until the people had rebuilt their homes.

Background Notes: The Hittites lived in the land that is now Turkey between 1900 B.C.–700 B.C. Every spring, they reenacted the slaying of Illuyankas to symbolize the rebirth of the earth after the long winter.

The Best Gift (Greek)

When the people of Athens finished building their beautiful city, they gathered on the hill overlooking the clear, blue ocean to decide what to name the city. Poseidon, god of the sea, raced over the waves in his chariot pulled by white horses and landed next to the people.

"Name the city after me!" he bellowed, waving his three-pronged trident.

A beautiful woman appeared next to Poseidon, wearing golden armor. "No," she said. "Name your lovely city after me!"

"Athena!" roared Poseidon. "You're the goddess of wisdom, art, and war," he said. "This city overlooks the sea. They should name it after me!"

"But the city is a work of art," replied Athena. "They should name it after me."

The people discussed this for a long time.

"Let us give you gifts, dear people," said Athena. "Name the city after the god whose gift is greatest."

The people agreed.

Poseidon stretched out his trident. "I give you safe passage across the seas," he said. "Your city will become wealthy through trade with other lands. What greater gift to a city can there be than wealth?"

"Thank you, Poseidon," replied the people. "That's a great gift!"

Athena pointed her spear at the ground and a twig lined with silvery leaves peeked out of the earth. "To the city, I give you this," she said.

Poseidon's laughter boomed across the land. "Ha!" he said. "I gave them wealth and you give them a stick?"

Athena smiled. "Yes," she said. "But this small stick will grow into a fine olive tree. And hundreds of trees like it will grow fruit that will feed the people. The oil from the fruit will light their homes and can be sold to other lands, bringing wealth to the city."

The people gazed across the clear water and down at the tiny twig. "Thank you both, for your generous gifts," they said. "Your gift of safe passage, Poseidon, is great. But without food to give us strength to build boats, and without oil to trade with other lands, your gift is useless. We will name our city after Athena, who has given us food, light, and something to trade."

Poseidon grabbed his trident, leaped into his chariot, and raced back across the waves. And Athena smiled.

Background Notes: The ancient Greeks believed their gods lived on Mount Olympus, a mythical mountain near Athens. They also believed the gods were active in humans' lives. This myth shows how the gods sometimes competed with each other for humans' affection.

Brothers Who Didn't Share (Roman)

Mars, the god of war, and the king's daughter, Rhea, had twin sons named Romulus and Remus. But Rhea's brother was jealous and threw the babies into the river. Instead of drowning, the babies floated along the river and came to rest at the edge of a meadow where a wolf mother was drinking.

The babies gazed up at the mother wolf and smiled. *What sweet humans*, thought the wolf mother as she carried them back to her den. There she raised the boys with her own wolf cubs.

When the boys grew older, a shepherd strolling through the meadow saw them. "That's Romulus and Remus—the sons of Mars," he said. And the shepherd took the twins from the wolf mother back to his home.

One day the shepherd told Romulus and Remus, "Good news! Your mean uncle was killed in a battle so it's safe for you to come out of hiding."

Romulus and Remus wanted to celebrate. "Let's build a city," said Romulus.

"But where?" asked Remus.

Romulus wanted the city here. Remus wanted it there. And they both wanted to be king of the new city.

Romulus plowed a line in the dirt where he wanted to build his city.

"No!" yelled Remus. "I want the city over there!" Remus felt jealous and jumped over the line—inside Romulus' boundaries.

Romulus was furious! He ran at Remus and killed him. Then he named the city "Rome" after himself and became its first king.

Sometimes people tell us that we are just like somebody else in our family. Romulus and Remus were like their relatives, too. They fought like their father, Mars—the god of war. And they were jealous, like their mean uncle. Too bad for poor Remus!

Background Notes: The Romans adopted gods from civilizations they conquered and renamed them. The Roman king of the gods (Jupiter) was the Greek god Zeus. The Roman god of war (Mars) was the Greek god Ares. The Roman god of the sea (Neptune) was the Greek god Poseidon. The Roman god of death (Pluto) was the Greek god Hades. The Roman goddess of beauty (Venus) was the Greek goddess Aphrodite.

WELCOME TO THE ANCIENT NEAR EAST

Station 2: Muddy Math

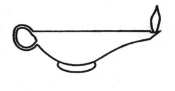

Have children locate the Near East on their map, color it green, and highlight the section of the timeline green that relates to the Near East. Cuneiform (que-NA-eh-form), one of the earliest forms of writing, was used in Mesopotamia in 3500 B.C. The name in Latin means "wedge" (*cuneus*) "shape" (*forma*). Cuneiform symbols look like wedges and hooks. Paper hadn't been invented yet, so people carved wet clay with a reed (a type of stiff grass). The end of the reed was set on the clay and turned from one side to another or dragged to form a "wedge" or "hook." When the clay hardened, the writing lasted a long time—unless the tablet broke!

The Code of Hammurabi (ha-mur-AH-bee) is a famous set of laws written in cuneiform during the reign of King Hammurabi of Babylon about 1700 B.C. Although there may have been other written laws that existed, this is the oldest set that has been found. The laws were put in a public place so people could read them and settle disputes.

The cuneiform language is complicated but the written numbers are easy to read. Let's make our own clay tablets and practice cuneiform math. For this station, you will need:

- These instructions

- One copy of *Jump Back* World Map of Ancient Cultures

- One copy of *Jump Back* Timeline

- Green crayons, marking pens, or pencils

- Modeling clay for each child to create a reusable "tablet" (approximately 6" × 8" and 1" thick)

- Slightly pointed writing instruments—pencils, plastic knives, or sticks—for each child

- Although clay can be flattened with hands, dowels or rolling pins make "erasing" easier

- "Muddy Math" handout (1 copy per child)

- One or two copies of "Muddy Math Problems" (fold to keep answers hidden)

Divide clay into chunks—one for each child in the group. As the adult leader reads these instructions, children can smooth and flatten clay into "tablets." Give each child a copy of the "Muddy Math" handout and have them practice carving numbers. Then have children "erase" their tablets by smoothing out the symbols and do calculations from the "Muddy Math Problems" sheet. Clay is reused by all groups.

TIPS FOR EXTRA FUN

- Use self-hardening clay and allow enough clay for each child to keep the tablet as a permanent historical record. Place the clay on newspaper to dry.

- Discuss clay tablets. Did different soil change the color of the tablets? In hot weather, would clay crack or make the writing look funny? What would school be like in Mesopotamia? Would students carry buckets of clay instead of binders? What if you set cuneiform homework outside and it rained? Let kids think up fun ways to compare school today with ancient times.

- Winners of math contests receive a small item—prize, candy, token, or ticket to save and buy a prize at end of day.

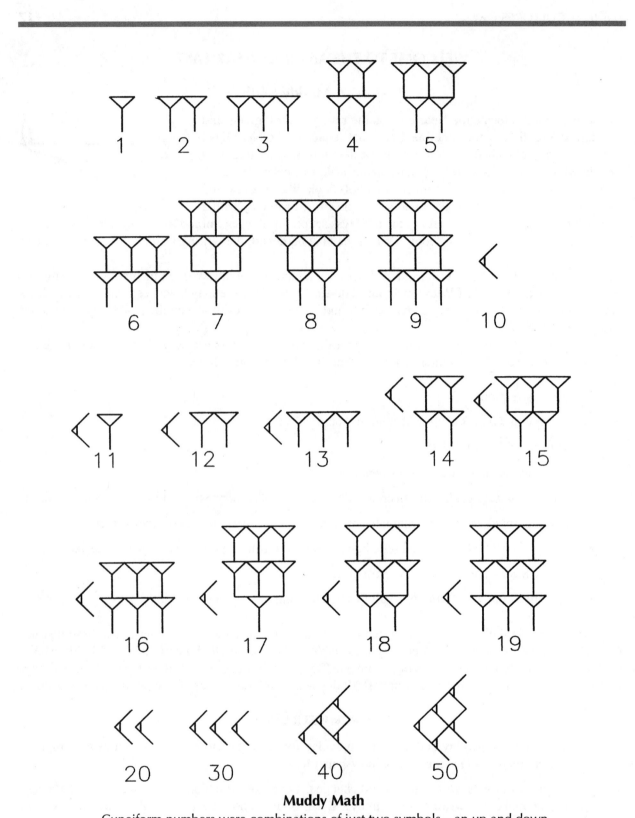

Muddy Math

Cuneiform numbers were combinations of just two symbols—an up and down wedge for the number "1" and a corner wedge for the number "10." This is how to write the numbers 1–50 in cuneiform.

PROBLEM

ANSWER

2 + 4 =

10 + 13 =

5 + 8 =

3 − 2 =

10 − 3 =

22 − 12 =

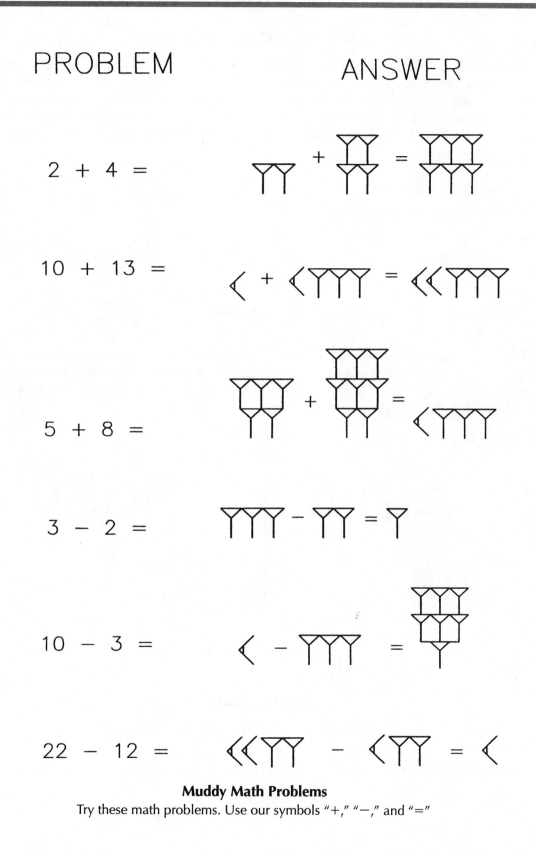

Muddy Math Problems

Try these math problems. Use our symbols "+," "−," and "="

Station 3. King David's Music Shop

King David was one of the greatest kings of the ancient Hebrew people. He ruled the kingdom of Israel in about 1100 B.C. and was an ancestor of Jesus Christ. David started out as a shepherd and played his harp while taking care of his father's sheep. Later he got a job playing harp for King Saul because David's music calmed the king's temper. Many of David's songs are written down in the Jewish Torah and in today's Christian Bible. A lyre is a type of small harp played throughout the ancient world. For each lyre you will need:

- These instructions
- 1 heavy cardboard-type paper plate
- 2 medium rubber bands (approximately 2½" long)
- Scissors
- Colored markers or crayons
- Copy of "Secrets in Scrolls" handout for each child

Decorate the paper plate with colorful designs. Cut four slits approximately ¼" deep on one side of the rim. Cut four corresponding rim slits on the other side of the plate. Slip one rubber band over two slits and stretch across the plate, attaching the other end to the two corresponding slits. Repeat with the second rubber band over the last sets of slits. Now play!

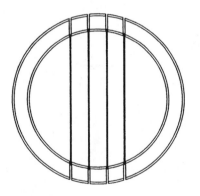

King David's Lyre

TIPS FOR EXTRA FUN

- Discuss how this early musical instrument is similar to and different from instruments we know today.
- Form a lyre band and sing songs. If you were David, would your music calm King Saul or make him laugh?

Secrets in Scrolls

The ancient Hebrew alphabet had no vowels, no punctuation, and no spaces between words. Without vowels, modern people can only guess what the language sounded like. Today small symbols underneath Hebrew letters tell you when to add a vowel sound.

Try writing the ancient Hebrew way. Use English letters, but don't use punctuation, spaces, or vowels, and write across the page from right to left as the ancient Hebrews did. Then try reading each other's writing. Roll up your paper and it becomes a "scroll." Ancient Hebrews made their scrolls from dried animal skin (parchment). We'll use paper. Try reading the following. Can you guess what it says?

HTRHTNSNVHHTDTRCDGGNNGBHTN

Hint #1: Reverse the order of the letters so you can read it left to right:

NTHBGNNGGDCRTDTHHVNSNTHRTH

Hint #2: TH = "the" (except for the last TH)

Hint #3: Try adding vowels between the consonants

Hint #4: Try sounding it out and adding spaces

Hint #5: It's the very first line from *Genesis,* the first book of the Jewish Torah and the Christian Old Testament.

Answer: In the beginning, God created the Heavens and the Earth.

WELCOME TO ANCIENT EGYPT

Station 4. Royal Cartouche Shop

Have children locate ancient Egypt on their map, color it blue, and highlight the parts of the timeline blue that relate to the Egyptian culture. A cartouche (car-TOOSH) is a special frame Egyptians placed around the names of kings, queens, and gods. No one else was allowed to use a cartouche. But we can. Let's write our names using hieroglyphics for the sounds of English letters. If there is more than one symbol for a sound, you  can choose which to use. Write from top to bottom and decorate the symbols and the frame with crayons, markers, or colored pencils. Write your name in English in the box at the bottom of the frame. Now don't you feel special? For this station you will need:

- These instructions

- One copy of *Jump Back* World Map of Ancient Cultures

- One copy of *Jump Back* Timeline

- Blue crayons, marking pens, or pencils and other assorted colors

- Copy of Cartouche Frame for each child

- Copy of "Hieroglyphics" handout for each child

Station 5. King Tut's House of Games

Many cultures in ancient Egypt and Africa played variations of the same board game. Called Oware, Mancala, Senat, or one of 200 other names, it may be the oldest board game in the world. Allow one game for every two children. For each game you will need:

- The bottom half of an empty egg carton (dozen) or a 12-cup muffin tin

- 2 paper cups

- 48 game pieces (pebbles, dry beans, beads, shells, seeds)

- Copy of "Dead or Alive?" handout for each child or 1 to read aloud

Oware is played by two people using seeds, stones, shells, or other small objects and a game board of 12 small bowls (6 bowls per person) and 2 cups (1 per person), called "mancalas." The object is to collect the most game pieces in your mancala.

Set the bottom part of an empty dozen-egg carton or muffin tin and the 2 empty cups (mancalas) between two players. Each player receives 24 game pieces. The separate mancala and one side (6 bowls) of the egg carton or muffin tin "belong" to each player. Decide who will begin the game, alphabetically by first name.

Start by dropping 24 pieces one at a time into your empty bowls on the right; first into "your" bowls and then continuing around the board counterclockwise until there are no more pieces. When you come to the end of the board and reach your own mancala, drop a stone into it. When you come to the other player's mancala, skip it and then continue to drop pieces into the next bowls, one at a time, until all pieces are gone.

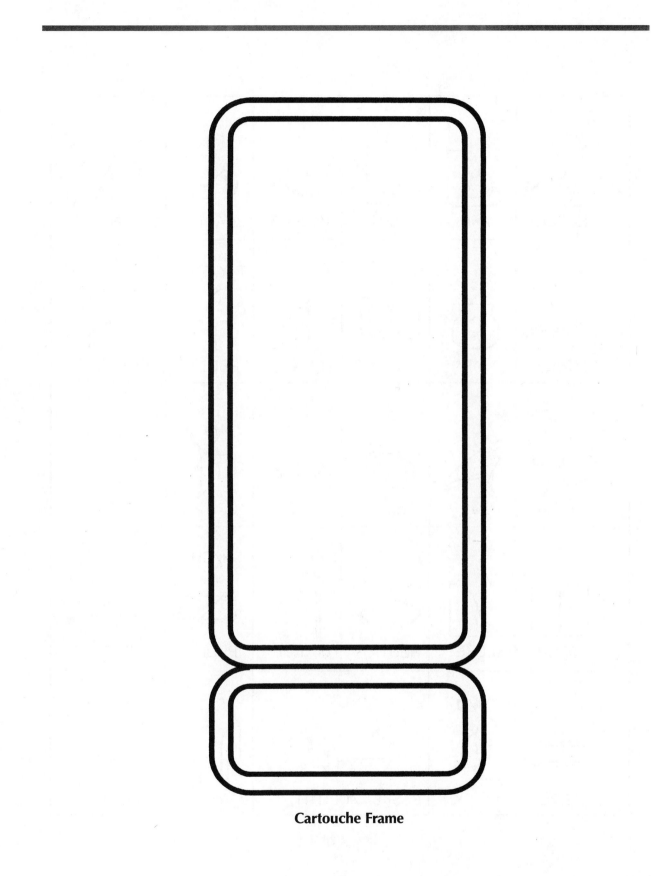

Cartouche Frame

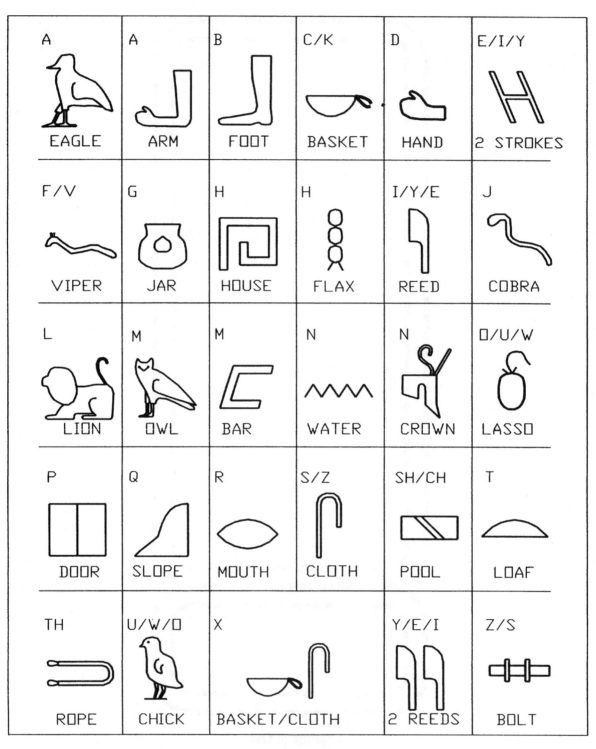

A — EAGLE	A — ARM	B — FOOT	C/K — BASKET	D — HAND	E/I/Y — 2 STROKES
F/V — VIPER	G — JAR	H — HOUSE	H — FLAX	I/Y/E — REED	J — COBRA
L — LION	M — OWL	M — BAR	N — WATER	N — CROWN	O/U/W — LASSO
P — DOOR	Q — SLOPE	R — MOUTH	S/Z — CLOTH	SH/CH — POOL	T — LOAF
TH — ROPE	U/W/O — CHICK	X — BASKET/CLOTH		Y/E/I — 2 REEDS	Z/S — BOLT

Hieroglyphics

If you drop your last piece into your own mancala, you get a second turn. Scoop up the pieces from any of your own bowls and drop them one-by-one into the next bowls. If you drop the last piece into an empty bowl on your side, take that stone and "capture" all the stones in the other player's bowl that is across from that bowl and place them in your mancala. Once you have made a capture or have run out of pieces to drop, it is the second player's turn.

The second player repeats this process. Then players take turns. The game ends when all 6 bowls of one person's side are empty. If you still have pieces in your own bowls at the end of the game, put the remaining pieces into your mancala. The player with the most pieces in his or her mancala wins.

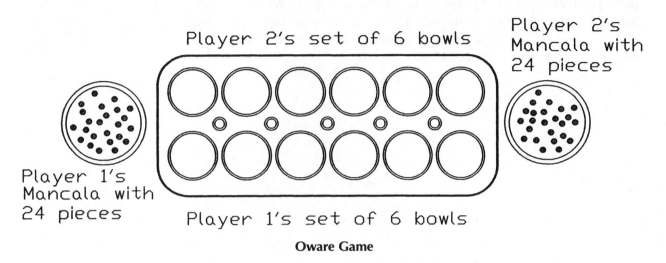

Oware Game

TIPS FOR EXTRA FUN

- Use dry beans, pebbles, beads, seeds, or any small objects for game pieces.

- Discuss how Oware helped people learn counting and mathematics.

- Discuss how this is similar to our modern games of backgammon and checkers.

- Read aloud "Dead or Alive?" or make copies to hand out.

Dead or Alive?

Egyptian pharaohs loved having their images painted on walls or made into bigger-than-life sculptures. Sometimes the portraits were made when the pharaoh was alive and sometimes they were made after he died. How can you tell if the pharaoh was dead or alive at the time?

Ancient Egyptians knew that the heart, essential for life, hung slightly to the left side of a person's body. So when Egyptian artists created a painting or sculpture of a living person, they showed the person with his left arm and left leg forward in a walking position. When the artist was showing a person who had died, he painted or carved the person's legs together and both arms either at his sides or crossed over his chest. So now, when you see an image of an ancient Egyptian, even if his eyes are open, you'll know whether that person was dead or alive.

WELCOME TO ANCIENT CHINA

Station 6. Emperor Qin's Army

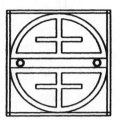

Have the children locate China on their map, color it red, and highlight the parts of the timeline red that relate to China. China is named after Qin Shi Huang (CHIN SHEE WAN), China's first emperor. About 210 B.C., Emperor Qin united the country under a single government. He made all weights, measurements, laws, writing, and currency the same and ordered the 6,700-kilometer-long Great Wall to be joined to protect the country. He was a cruel emperor and only ruled for 15 years, but his reign began a 2,000-year form of government.

Emperor Qin ordered a tomb built for himself with an army of more than 7,000 clay soldiers to guard it. In 1974, peasants found the army while digging for a well. Each figure is different. Some ride horses. Some stand in wooden chariots. Others carry spears or bows and arrows to protect the emperor throughout eternity.

Near the army is a mound that contains his tomb. The tomb has not been opened yet because scientists are worried air will destroy the delicate treasures inside. Written records say that Emperor Qin's tomb contains whole palaces and rare gems, that the ceiling was inlaid with pearls to look like stars, that the walls and floor were lined with bronze to keep out water, and that there is even a lake filled with mercury. The records also say that crossbows inside the tomb will automatically shoot anyone who opens it.

Today we'll recreate Emperor Qin's clay army. Everyone gets to make their own clay soldiers to line in battle formation. By the end of the day, we'll have an army to guard Emperor Qin. For this station you will need:

- These instructions
- One copy of *Jump Back* World Map of Ancient Cultures
- One copy of *Jump Back* Timeline
- Red crayons, markers, or pencils
- Molding clay for each child to make a small figure. (Clay will NOT be reused.)
- No handout (clay figure is a souvenir at the end of the day)

TIPS FOR EXTRA FUN

- Use self-hardening clay for more permanence.
- Make sure kids etch their names on the figures.
- Don't make figures too tall or they may not stand.
- Encourage children to make horses and chariots as well as soldiers.

Station 7. Calligraphy Card Shop

Chinese calligraphy means "good writing" and dates back to 3500 B.C. Before paper was invented, ancient Chinese wrote on tortoise shells. Decorated paper scrolls have been used since about 300 B.C. Chinese words are made up of characters that started out as pictures. To read Chinese, start at the top right hand side of the page, go down to the bottom, then to the top of the next column on the left; back down to the bottom and up again to the next column on the left. Top to bottom and right to left! At this station you will need:

- These instructions
- Copy of "Calligraphy Scroll" handout for each child or several samples, and a sheet of plain white paper (8½" × 14") cut in half lengthwise for each child
- Black paint
- Paintbrushes
- Water
- Paper towels
- Newspaper to cover tables
- Copy of "Calligraphy Counting" handout for each child
- Watercolor paint sets (optional)
- Ribbon cut in 8" lengths (optional)

TIPS FOR EXTRA FUN

- Children can either paint directly on the calligraphy sample or use it as a guide.
- If time allows, decorate scrolls with a watercolor landscape or figure. Allow at least one paint set for every two children.
- After the paint dries, roll and tie with a ribbon.

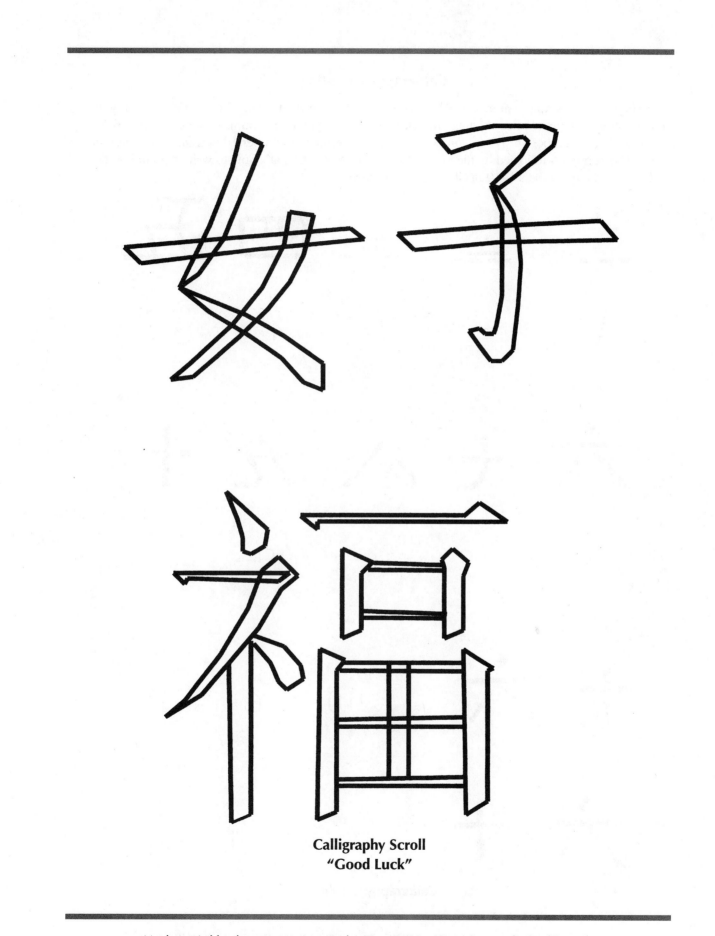

Calligraphy Scroll
"Good Luck"

Calligraphy Counting

There are ten Chinese numbers. When you place a number after the Chinese number 10, you add the two numbers together. For example, the number 10 followed by the number 6 means 10 + 6. That's how to write the number 16. When you place a number before the number 10 you multiply that number by ten. The number 6 followed by the number 10 means 6 × 10. That's how to write the number 60.

Here are the numbers 1–10 in Chinese calligraphy.

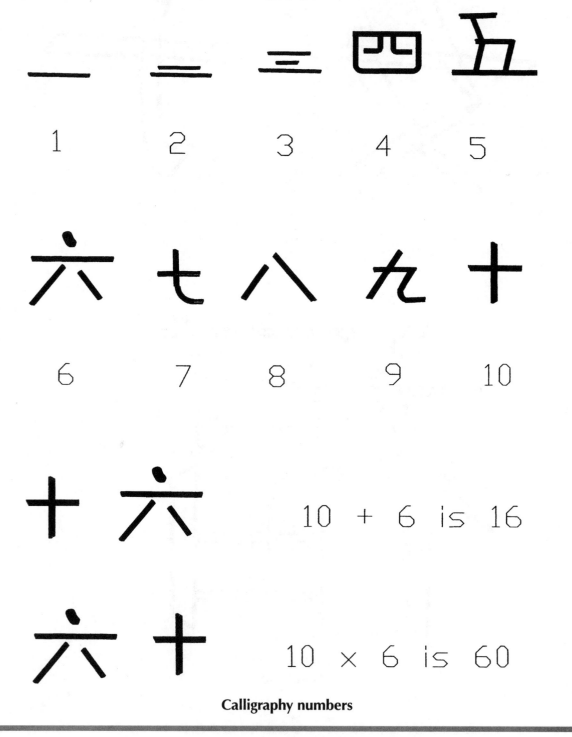

Calligraphy numbers

WELCOME TO ANCIENT GREECE

Station 8. Greek Sandal Shop

Have children locate Greece on their map, color the star at Athens yellow, and highlight the parts of the timeline that relate to the Greek empire. Children will make sandals at this station. You will need:

- These instructions

- One copy of *Jump Back* World Map of Ancient Cultures

- One copy of *Jump Back* Timeline

- Yellow crayons, markers, or pencils

- Poster board or cardboard—not too heavy as children need to cut out patterns with scissors. Allow one piece of cardboard approximately 8½" × 11" for each child.

- Sandal patterns (several)

- Pencils

- Scissors

- Several hole punches or large nails

- Yarn, heavy string, or twine—about 3' for each sandal

Cut out pattern pieces for the soles onto poster board. Punch four holes at each toe where indicated. Punch two holes at each heel where indicated. Cut two 3-foot lengths of yarn.

Thread the yarn UP through the two end toe holes. Then cross the yarn over to the second set of toe holes and thread back DOWN. Turn the sole over and even up the ends of yarn. Thread yarn back UP through each hole at the heel. Repeat for both sandals. Slip the foot into the laced "toe." Wrap straps around the ankle several times and tie.

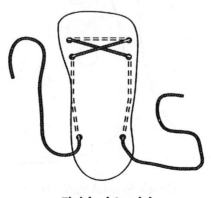

Finished Sandal

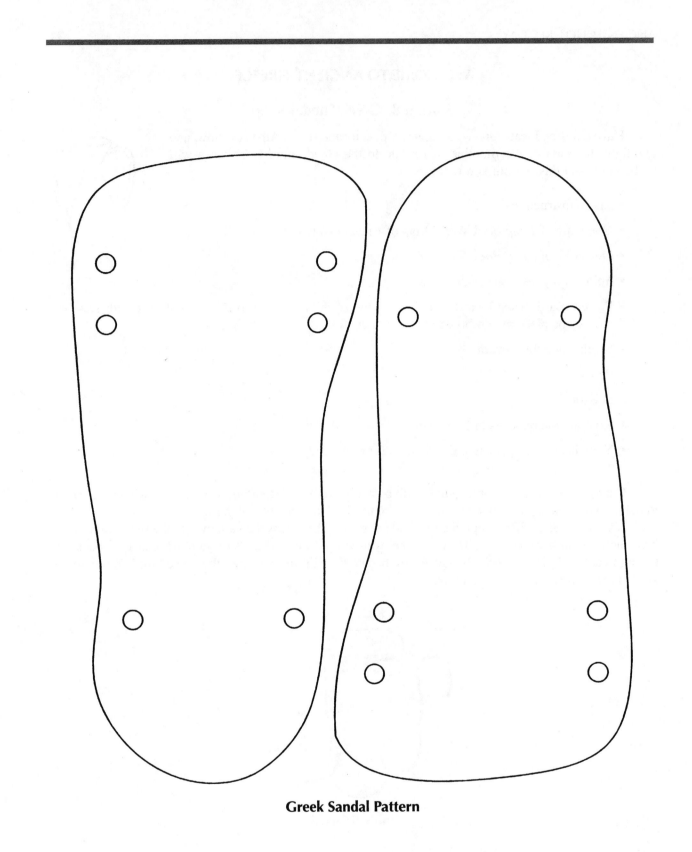

Greek Sandal Pattern

TIPS FOR EXTRA FUN

- Use colorful poster board. Make sure the color side is up.

- Wind the straps up toward the knee for an "ancient" look.

- Most Greeks wore sandals made from leather, sometimes with wooden soles. Lead a discussion about wood soles—comfort, durability, splinters.

- Ahead of time, make a "sandal" using a thin piece of wood instead of cardboard. Let children take turns trying it on.

Station 9. Alexander's Great Library

Children will write their names using the Greek Alphabet handout. For this station you will need:

- These instructions
- Copy of "Greek Alphabet" handout for each child
- Pencils or pens

TIPS FOR EXTRA FUN

- Try writing your friends' names.

- Mix papers and "read" the names.

- Discuss which letters are like our letters, which letters "look" like ours but sound different, and which letters are completely different from ours.

Capital Letter	Small letter	Name	Sound
A	α	alpha	a
B	β	beta	b
Γ	γ	gamma	g
Δ	δ	delta	d
E	ε	epsilon	e (as in "bed")
Z	ζ	zeta	z
H	η	eta	e (as in "hay")
Θ	θ	theta	th (as in "thanks")
I	ι	iota	i
K	κ	kappa	k
Λ	λ	lambda	l
M	μ	mu	m
N	ν	nu	n
≅	ξ	xi	x
O	o	omicron	o (as in "hot")
Π	π	pi	p
P	ρ	rho	r
Σ	σ	sigma	s
T	τ	tau	t
Y	υ	upsilon	u
Φ	φ	phi	ph
X	χ	chi	kh
Ψ	ψ	psi	ps
Ω	ω	omega	o (as in "home")

Greek Alphabet

Think about how your name sounds. Then write your name using the Greek letters. Remember to use a capital for the first letter and small letters for the rest of your name.

WELCOME TO ANCIENT ROME

Station 10. Julian Calendar

Have the children locate Rome on their map, color the star purple, and highlight the part of the timeline purple that relates to Rome. At this station you will need:

- These instructions
- One copy of *Jump Back* World Map of Ancient Cultures
- One copy of *Jump Back* Timeline
- Purple crayons, marking pens, or pencils, and assorted colors to decorate calendars
- Calendar template copied back-to-back (3 sheets for each child)
- Optional colored cover sheets for each child
- Stapler
- Scissors (or precut the calendar templates in half)
- Copy of current calendar as reference for dates

A "solar year" is the amount of time it takes the earth to go completely around the sun (365¼ days). Early Romans used a calendar with only ten months (304 days). That made life confusing because without enough days in the year, the spring season didn't always start during the same month each year. In about 715 B.C., Emperor Pompilius (Pom-PILL-e-us) added two months to the Roman calendar. Although this new calendar had 12 months, the year was only 355 days long—still not long enough. It, too, became confusing.

In 46 B.C., Julius Caesar again changed the calendar. This new calendar, known as the "Julian calendar" in his honor, had 365 days and was used for 1,500 years. To get the calendar back in line with the sun, the first year his calendar was used had 445 days. The Romans called that year "the year of confusion"!

The Julian calendar was still off and by A.D. 1580 it was off by ten days. So in 1582, Pope Gregory XIII revised the calendar again, adding one day every four years. It is called the "Georgian calendar" in his honor and is the calendar we still use today. Today we will make a calendar using the Roman names of the month:

Januarius	**Februarius**	**Martius**	**Aprilis**	**Maius**	**Junius**
Julius	**Augustus**	**September**	**October**	**November**	**December**

Make one calendar using 3 full sheets of paper copied back-to-back or 6 sheets copied on one side and a cover page. Cut the pages in half and staple them together. Use a current calendar or one for next year as a guide for dates—but use the Roman names for fun. Children can decorate the cover.

Sunday	Monday	Tuesday	Wednesday	Thursday	Friday	Saturday

Sunday	Monday	Tuesday	Wednesday	Thursday	Friday	Saturday

Roman Calendar Template

Station 11. Mosaic Masterpieces

Romans decorated their buildings with murals. Sometimes, they painted wet plaster with bright colors, called "fresco" painting. Romans were also known for their "mosaics"—pictures made out of small pieces of colored stone, glass, or pottery. To make mosaics, you will need:

- 1 large poster board for each group or a length of butcher paper—about 10' long. Plan a scene that can be sketched out—people or landscape with sun and hills, valley, river, trees.

- Precut pieces of colored paper approximately 1" square. Separate colors. Have enough to cover all poster boards or the entire mural.

- Glue or glue sticks—enough for each child.

- Small boxes to keep color squares separate.

- Copy of "Roman Numerals" handout for each child

TIPS FOR EXTRA FUN

- Do this as a group project—one large mural for all groups to add on to as they rotate through the station, or one poster board mural per group. If making one large mural, have each group work on one section—completing, for example, a tree, or one section of the sky, so that groups can later clearly see their section.

- Make this mosaic a scene from Roman life, a portrait of a person, picture of an animal, or an outdoor scene.

- Murals can be used as background for group photos at the end of the day.

- Have extra paper and scissors handy for more mosaic pieces.

- If time allows, read and do the activity on the "Roman Numerals" handout.

Roman Numerals

Romans could write every number from one to one million using only seven symbols (we use ten). Although that made it easy to learn the symbols, sometimes large numbers took a lot of writing. For example, the number 837 was: DCCCXXXVII.

Today we still use Roman numberals. Look for Roman numerals on clocks, at the corners of old buildings, and to number book chapters. This is how to write Roman numerals:

I	**one**	**VI**	**six**	**L**	**fifty**
II	**two**	**VII**	**seven**	**C**	**one hundred**
III	**three**	**VIII**	**eight**	**D**	**five hundred**
IV	**four**	**IX**	**nine**	**M**	**one thousand**
V	**five**	**X**	**ten**		

Try writing out today's date in Roman numerals, or try writing your birthday, your age, or your phone number.

WELCOME TO ANCIENT MESOAMERICA

Station 12. Chocolate Checkers

Have the children locate Mesoamerica on their map, color it orange, and highlight the parts of the timeline orange that relate to Mesoamerica. For this station you will need:

- These instructions

- One copy of *Jump Back* World Map of Ancient Cultures

- One copy of *Jump Back* Timeline

- Orange crayons, markers, or colored pencils

- 1 copy of bul game board for every two players

- 1 die for every two players

- Wrapped chocolate candies—5 per child

- Copy of "My, Oh My! Mayan Math!" handout for each child

Mayans didn't have coins or paper money—they used cacao beans. Cacao beans are also used to make chocolate. Mayans played a board game called "bul" that was similar to checkers. Today, we'll play bul using chocolate game pieces. The winner gets to eat his winnings!

Mayans made game boards on the ground by placing 15 kernels of corn in a row. The 14 spaces in between the kernels were the board. They used another 4 kernels with a burn mark on one side as dice. When the kernels were tossed, the number of burned sides up told the players how many spaces to move. Today we'll use dice.

Pair up with 1 game board and 1 die per couple and 5 wrapped chocolate candies each. Roll the die to see who starts—highest number goes first. Players start with a single game piece at opposite ends of the board. If you are the first person to roll the die, move your chocolate that number of spaces from your side of the board toward the other side. Take a second roll and move again to end your turn. The second player rolls and takes two turns. When you reach the other side of the board, you reenter the board where you started, as if the board goes in a circle.

The object of the game is to land on a space occupied by the other player. That other player's game piece becomes your "captive." You then change direction and "drag" the captive back to your end of the board. When you reach your side, the captive is "dead." You keep the captive's chocolate and reenter your piece into play. The game continues until all of one player's pieces are dead (or until the time is up).

TIPS FOR EXTRA FUN

- Eat your captured enemy immediately! Savor the victory.

- Discuss how much chocolate it might cost to "buy" things at a Mayan market.

- Cacao beans were made into a chocolate drink used only during religious ceremonies. One hundred cacao beans make about 25 cups of chocolate. Think about that next time you drink hot chocolate or chocolate milk.

- If time allows, read aloud "My, Oh My! Mayan Math!" Discuss how the Mayan 20-based numbering system is different from ours, which is based on 10s.

PLAYER #1

PLAYER #2

Bul Game Board

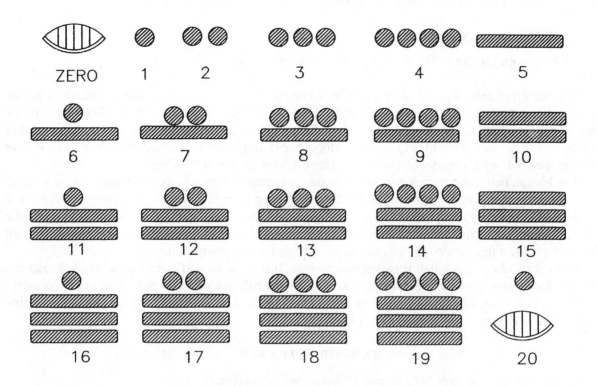

Numbers 1 through 20. Our numbers are based on 10s; Mayan numbers were based on 20. Numbers over 20 were written in powers of 20, from top to bottom.

Example: The number 53 was written from top to bottom:

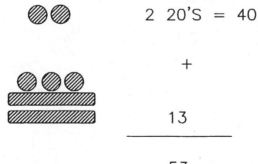

2 20'S = 40

+

13
_____

53

My, Oh My! Mayan Math!

Station 13. Pok-A-Tok

Children will play the Mayan game of pok-a-tok. At this station you will need:

- One ball for every two children

- Copy of the handout "The Winning Twins" for each child

Mayans loved ball games. They even believed the gods played ball. Almost every Mayan city had its own ball court, about the size of a football field but shaped like a capital letter "I." The object of the game was to get a hard rubber ball about the size of a volleyball through a high hoop. The players had to keep the ball in the air but could only use their elbow, wrist, thigh, arms, hip, and shoulders. No hands or feet! The hard ball weighed about 8 pounds, so players wore plenty of padding.

The Mayan ball game represented life after death. Sometimes they forced captured enemy soldiers to play the game as a way to reenact a battle. Then the losing team was sacrificed to the gods. A Mayan myth tells of hero twins who played ball with the gods and won. By playing ball, Mayans reenacted the story and identified themselves with those ancient heroes. Also, because the ball was kept in constant motion in the air, it represented the sun and moon's constant movement in the sky.

Pair off children with 1 ball between two players. If there is an odd number, the whole group can play in a circle using a single ball. One person bounces the ball to another person. That person must hit the ball back or to a third person without using hands or feet. Keep trying. Remember—the losing Mayan team lost more than the game. They lost their lives!

TIPS FOR EXTRA FUN

- Read the Mayan myth "The Winning Twins" before playing the game.

- Think how the Mayan ball game compares with our games of basketball (hoop), soccer (no hands), football (padding), volleyball (keep the ball in the air), and other games.

- Imagine hitting a very hard and heavy ball 15 feet above your head through a small hoop!

The Winning Twins (Mayan Myth of Sacrifice)

The Mayan universe was made up of three parts—the Upperworld, Earth, and the Underworld. The gods lived in the Upperworld and the Underworld. Only humans lived on Earth. One day, the human twins, Hunahpu (hoo-nah-POOH) and Xbalanque (sh-bah-LAHN-kay) traveled to the Underworld where the gods of death lived.

"You must play a game of ball," roared the gods of death, "or you shall die!"

The twins played many ball games with the gods of death but could never win.

"They will not be satisfied until we are dead," said Hunahpu and Xbalanque. So they leaped into fire and died.

The death gods were happy. They threw Hunahpu and Xbalanque's bones into the river. But the twins' sacrifice gave them special powers and they were reborn as the sun and moon.

"Let's take revenge on the gods of death," said Hunahpu and Xbalanque. They returned to the Underworld disguised as actors to entertain the gods of death with magic.

"Watch this," the twins said to the gods, as they killed a dog and brought it back to life.

The gods of death watched the dog wag its tail, happy to be alive again.

"Good trick," said the gods of death.

"Here's another one," said the twins. They sacrificed a man and brought him back to life.

The man thanked the twins over and over for bringing him back to life.

"Very good trick," said the gods of death.

"Then you'll like this one, too," said Xbalanque. And he killed Hunahpu and brought him back to life.

The gods of death were amazed. Everyone the twins brought back to life was so happy to be alive again. "Kill us and bring us back to life," said the gods of death. "We want to be happy, too!"

"As you please," said Hunahpu and Xbalanque. The twins killed the gods of death but did *not* bring them back to life. Their plan worked. They had won.

Background Notes: The setting and rising sun symbolizes the twins' journey to and return from the Underworld and their victory over death. This story also shows the Mayan belief in rebirth through sacrifice and explains their interest in the ball game and astronomy. This and other Mayan stories that had been retold for centuries were finally written down in the 16th century in a book called *Popul-Vuh* (POH-pole VOO).

END THE DAY AS A GROUP

Station 14. Atop Mt. Olympus

The Olympic games started in Greece in 776 B.C. They were held every four years and lasted for five days. All wars stopped during the Olympics and winning athletes were treated as heroes. The Greeks believed the gods lived on Mt. Olympus, so they held the games at a religious center called "Olympia." The very first Olympic games only had one event—a race approximately 200 yards long. Today's events will be the long jump (jump over chalk marks), the sprint (50-yard dash), and discus (plastic throwing discs). These events should be done outside. For this station you will need the following:

- Tape measurer

- Chalk

- Plastic throwing discs

- Paper and pencil for scoring

Long Jump: Measure and mark out 5' at 6" intervals. Have children line up at one end and see how far they can go without a running leap. If time allows, have them then try it with a running start. Note the winning jumpers.

Sprint: Measure off 50 yards and mark with chalk. If the group is small, on "go" everyone can start at once. If the group is larger than 6–8, pair off in twos. Note the winning runner(s).

Discus: Pair off with one plastic throwing disc for two children. Toss the disc back and forth giving each child a chance to miss three times. The winning players from each team pair off and compete—the last one remaining wins the event. Note the winner.

TIPS FOR EXTRA FUN

- Everyone can do one event together before moving to the next event.

- Alternatively, all children can rotate through the events in their groups. After all have participated, announce the winner from each group for each event.

- Winners receive small prizes (a laurel wreath, candy, certificate, blue ribbon).

- Keep chalk handy to redraw markers if needed.

Station 15. Make-Your-Own Rosetta Stone

Modern people didn't always know how to read ancient writing. Egyptian hieroglyphs were a mystery until a black stone was discovered in A.D. 1799 near Rosetta, Egypt. The stone had writing in Greek, Egyptian hieroglyphics, and another Egyptian language. A French researcher, Jean Champollion, translated the Greek and the second Egyptian writing. Both writings said the same thing! He knew that the hieroglyphics probably also said the same thing, so he matched the symbols with the words he knew and translated the hieroglyphics.

The phrase "Rosetta Stone" has come to mean a key that unlocks a secret. Today you learned to write several kinds of ancient numbers. Fill in the chart with the ancient numbers you learned and you'll have your own "Rosetta Number Stone"!

Language	Number 1	Number 2	Number 3	Number 4	Number 5	Number 6	Number 7	Number 8	Number 9	Number 10
English	1	2	3	4	5	6	7	8	9	10

Rosetta Number Stone

Station 16. Ancient Snack Shack

This station combines group photographs, snacks, and assembling souvenir booklets (see Chapter 1). Use the Roman mosaic as a backdrop for photos and don't forget—costumes and props make it more fun for everyone. At this station you will need:

- The Roman mosaic
- Tape or tacks to attach mural to wall (or children can hold the mural)
- Camera and film
- Costumes and/or props
- Colored construction paper
- Stapler
- Crayons, colored markers

Here are some ideas for simple treats:

- Pita bread—flat bread similar to bread eaten in the Near East, Egypt, Greece, and Rome
- Yogurt—plain or with honey, nuts, dried fruit (Greece, Egypt, Rome)
- Grapes and raisins (Egypt, Greece, Rome)
- Olives (Greece)
- Fruit—dipped in honey (Mayan)
- Oranges, tangerines (China)
- Crisp rice marshmallow bars—exploded rice is similar to our crisped rice cereal (China)
- Tortillas—plain or rolled up with butter, sugar, and cinnamon (Mayan)
- Popcorn—plain or drizzled with honey (Mayan)
- Chocolate candies—(Mayan)
- Drinks: Hot chocolate or chocolate milk (Mayan), tea (China), grape juice (Roman)
- Cups, napkins, plates, and utensils, as needed

TIPS FOR EXTRA FUN

- The more elaborate the costumes and props, the more the fun!
- Encourage kids to come to the event already dressed in costume—adults, too! Remember: Many cultural groups are represented today.
- Have music playing in the background.
- Make copies of the photo for everybody.
- SMILE!

Chapter 3

Native American Culture Day

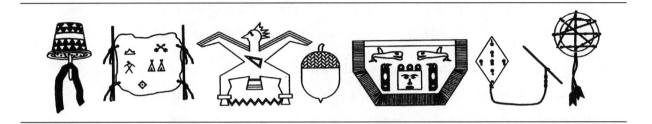

Welcome to Native American Culture Day. During this day of fun, children rotate through stations sampling Native American cultures. This is not a study of specific tribes but rather touches on the connection between environment and lifestyle. Each region includes "WATCH Facts"—*where, what's there, and weather* (W), foods the people *ate* (A), *tribes* (T), *clothing* (C), and *housing* (H), plus "something to think about." These WATCH Facts can be used as a springboard to discuss the relationship between resources and lifestyle. On the same sheet are "Notable Natives," which highlight an important person from that region. Each region also includes one separate reproducible legend and two hands-on activities.

When planning your Native American Culture Day, pick stations from each of the seven regions. The Map of North American Regions—colored throughout the day as introduced—should be part of the souvenir booklet. Make sure the map is included even if the first station of each region is not part of your event. The stations and activities for Native American Culture Day are:

Start the Day as a Group

Station 1. Tribal Council (Introduce Geographical Regions, Gathering Bags, Grouping, and Nametags)

Into the Woods—Welcome to the Eastern Woodlands

Station 2. Peach Pits and Wigwams (WATCH Facts/Notable Natives; Iroquois Dice Game)

Station 3. Catch a Dream ("Legend of Spider Woman"; Chippewa Dream Catchers)

Five Civilized Tribes—Welcome to the Southeast

Station 4. Shuttlecock Toss (WATCH Facts/Notable Natives; make Shuttlecocks)

Station 5. Shake, Rattle, and Roll ("Legend of Possum"; Yo-Gourd Rattles)

Where the Buffalo Roam—Welcome to the Plains

Station 6. Apache Scrolls (WATCH Facts/Notable Natives; Apache Scrolls)

Station 7. Buffalo Hunter Training ("Legend of the Bluebonnet Flower"; Hoop and Pole Game)

Pueblo People—Welcome to the Southwest

Station 8. Ceremonies in Sand (WATCH Facts/Notable Natives; Sand Painting)

Station 9. Masks and Myths ("Legend of the Five Worlds"; Kachina Masks)

Hills and Valleys—Welcome to the Great Basin, Plateau, and California

Station 10. Winning Spinners (WATCH Facts/Notable Natives; Spinners)

Station 11. Treetops to Tabletops ("How Coyote Made Man"; Board Game)

Totems and Tales—Welcome to the Northwest Coast

Station 12. Blanket Weavers (WATCH Facts/Notable Natives; Chilkat Blankets)

Station 13. Fun with Frontlets ("How Raven Stole the Heavens"; Fontlets)

Mukluk Mania—Welcome to the Subarctic and Arctic

Station 14. Bundles of Sticks (WATCH Facts/Notable Natives; Stick Game)

Station 15. Igloos and Icicles ("Legend of Sedna, Maiden of the Sea"; Ring and Pin Game)

End the Day as a Group

Station 16. Pow Wow Wow Dance

Station 17. Potlatch (Snacks, Group Photos, Souvenir Booklet)

NAMETAGS

Use the following tribes for group nametags or think up some of your own:
Yurok, Shasta, Washoe, Shoshone, Maido, Pomo, Ute, Miwok, Chumash, Nez Percé, Spokane, Walla Walla, Yakima, Klamath, Modoc, Tlingit, Bella Bella, Chinook, Tillamook, Choctaw, Pensacola, Cherokee, Seminole, Calusa, Ojibwa, Winnebago, Fox, Peoria, Kickapoo, Miami, Shawnee, Ottawa, Algonquin, Mohawk, Onondaga, Mohegan, Yellowknife, Beaver

COSTUME IDEAS

Kids and adults will have more fun if they dress in costume. Try to avoid stereotypes and, certainly, the emphasis is on native peoples, not cowboys or colonialists. Clothing is discussed in each set of WATCH Facts. Many native groups, however, wore blanket-type wraps over other clothing. Simple props might include beads, face painting, moccasins, and sandals.

START THE DAY AS A GROUP

Station 1. Tribal Council

All children assemble at this station. They are placed into their rotation groups and given nametags and instructions while making gathering bags. Using the *Jump Back* Map of North American Regions as a guide, explain the regions and hand out copies. Children will color regions as they move through the stations. For this station you will need:

- These instructions

- A large map of North America

- Copy of *Jump Back* Map of North American Regions for each child

- Items to make gathering bags (see Chapter 1)

TIPS FOR EXTRA FUN

- Try the public library for Native American music to help get kids in the mood.

- Ask children who have dressed in costume to explain what culture they represent.

- Provide costumes or accessories for kids to try on or wear throughout the day—beads, face paint, etc.—or provide costumes at the first station of each region to wear only at that station.

Parfleche Gathering Bag

A "parfleche" held food and small items when people traveled. They were used by many groups of Native Americans and came in different shapes (packets, envelopes, cylinders). Children will use a "parfleche" today for papers, but will need a second bag to collect bulkier craft projects (see Chapter 1). Suggest they decorate gathering bags with map locations or something to represent one of the cultures. For each parfleche, you will need:

- These instructions

- One large brown paper grocery bag or 18" × 24" construction paper

- String or yarn—2 pieces, 10" long each

- Scissors, hole punch, colored markers

- A second plastic or paper grocery bag for crafts

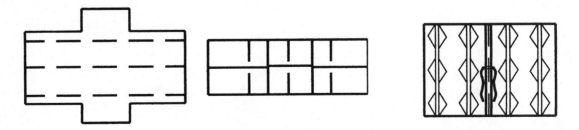

Fold on dotted lines, decorate, and tie

Parfleche

Cut open paper bag at back seam, remove bottom, and cut sides as shown. Decorate plain side with colored markers and mark name on the front. Turn paper face down and fold in half lengthwise to mark the center. Open and fold top edge down and bottom edge up to meet center crease. Fold in half widthwise to mark the center in that direction and open. Fold right edge and left edge to center crease. Punch holes at each edge of the opening and tie a string through each hole.

TIPS FOR EXTRA FUN

- Crumple the paper bag after decorating it but before assembly to give it a "rawhide" look.

- Instead of grocery bags, use thick paper in a light color so designs will show.

- Do this activity at the end of the day instead of making a stapled "booklet."

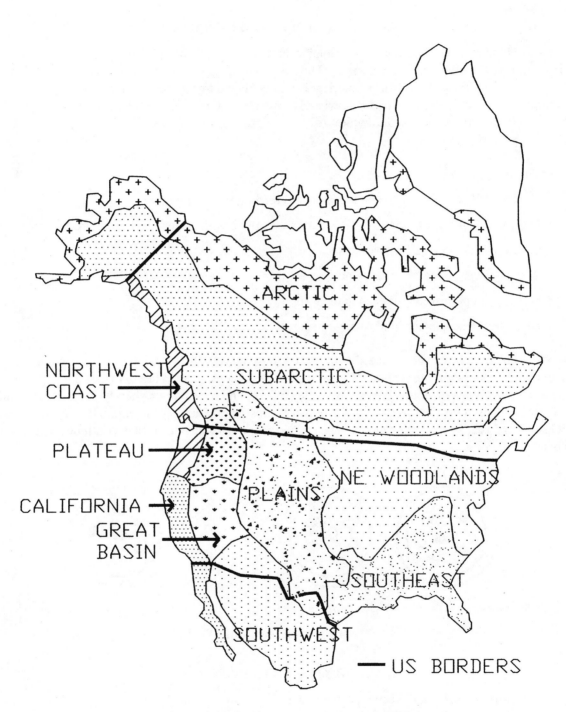

NORTHWEST
COAST

PLATEAU

CALIFORNIA

GREAT
BASIN

ARCTIC

SUBARCTIC

NE WOODLANDS

PLAINS

SOUTHEAST

SOUTHWEST

— US BORDERS

Jump Back Map of North American Regions

INTO THE WOODS—WELCOME TO THE EASTERN WOODLANDS

Station 2. Peach Pits and Wigwams

Read aloud the WATCH Facts and Notable Natives. Locate the Eastern Woodlands region on the map and color it green. Then play the Iroquois Dice Game. Dice games were played throughout North America. Iroquois played this game at a midwinter ceremony using a decorated wooden bowl and 6 peach pits. One side of each pit was burned black; the other side was left white. Allow one game for every 2–4 players. At this station you will need:

- These instructions

- Copies of WATCH Facts/Notable Natives to read aloud and hand out

- Copy of *Jump Back* Map of North American Regions with eastern region colored green

- Green pencils, crayons, or markers

- A heavy paper plate for each game

- 6 dried pumpkin seeds for each game

- Black felt pens, pencils, and paper for scoring

With a black felt pen, color one side of each pumpkin seed. Place seeds on plate. Decide who will play first alphabetically by first name. The second person keeps score. The first person grasps the plate with both hands, holds it about 4" above the table or floor, and sets it down sharply so the seeds "jump." If 5–6 of the seeds show the same color, the player scores 1 point and plays again. He continues playing until less than 5 seeds are the same color. The second player takes his turn. Play continues until one person reaches 30 points.

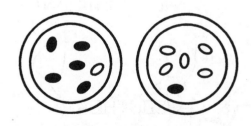

5-6 same color = 1 point and another turn   2-4 same color = no point

Iroquois Dice Game

TIPS FOR EXTRA FUN

- Let everyone make and keep their own game.

- Use a different color for each seed and assign a point value to each color.

WATCH Facts (Eastern Woodlands)

Where: Locate the Eastern Woodlands region on the map and color it green.

Weather: Mild in spring, summer, and fall; cold in winter.

What's There: Wood; leather from animal skins.

Ate: Moose, deer, ducks; fish from lakes and Atlantic Ocean. Wild nuts, berries, fruit; grew corn and tobacco. Wild plants and crops died in winter.

Tribes Included: Ojibwa (also called Chippewa), Winnebago, Fox, Peoria, Illinois, Kickapoo, Miami, Shawnee, Mohawk, Seneca, Delaware, Abnaki, Nipmuc, Mohegan, Iroquois, Mohawk, Oneida, Onondaga, and Cayuga.

Clothing: Men and women wore moose or deerskin leather loincloths (like an apron) and shirts.

Housing: Portable so people could follow animals for hunting—animal skin tents or "wigwams" (a wooden frame of bent trees covered with long strips of bark).

Something to think about: If you leave the hide on an animal's shoulders and front legs in one piece when skinning it, you have instant sleeves.

Notable Natives: Hole-in-the-Day

Hole-in-the-Day's (Bug-o-nay-ki-shig) father was an Ojibway war chief. But Hole-in-the-Day became a diplomat. Ojibway custom allowed men to have more than one wife, so Hole-in-the-Day married daughters of chiefs from nearly every Ojibway band. This gave him influence over the Ojibway nation.

When his father died, Hole-in-the-Day negotiated treaties with the U.S. government and was in favor of accepting some of the white man's customs. In exchange for his support, the U.S. government gave Hole-in-the-Day land, wealth, and personal favors. Many of the other chiefs began to resent Hole-in-the-Day and no longer acknowledged him as their leader. At the same time, a change of ideas within the U.S. government meant that Hole-in-the-Day no longer received personal favors. Once he was outside of the U.S. government system, he understood how much he had benefited personally and told his people. They called him a betrayer.

Finally, when other chiefs took over Ojibway leadership, members of Hole-in-the-Day's own tribe killed him. Despite the sad end to his life, Hole-in-the-Day had been recognized as a great leader both by his own people and the U.S. government. He is known for his short career as a brilliant diplomat who tried to balance the rights and lifestyle of his people with keeping a friendly relationship with the United States government.

Station 3. Catch a Dream

At this station children will make Chippewa dream catchers. Read aloud "Legend of Spider Woman" before or while making dream catchers. You will need the following:

- These instructions
- "Legend of Spider Woman" to read aloud and hand out
- One 6" paper plate (medium thickness) for each dream catcher
- One 4' length of string, colored twine, or yarn for each dream catcher
- 8–10 colored beads for each dream catcher
- 2 feathers for each dream catcher
- Scissors, hole punch, nails, tape

Poke a hole in the middle of a 6" paper plate with a nail. Cut out the center of the plate, leaving a 1-inch wide unbroken border. Discard the center. Using a hole punch, make 8 holes equidistant around the frame.

Tape the ends of a 4' long piece of string, twine, or yarn for easy threading. Thread the string through the bottom hole, leaving approximately 6" hanging. Thread a bead onto the top end of the string and pass the string through the top hole so it crosses the center of the frame. Thread another bead and pass the string back through a hole on the opposite side of the frame—again crossing through the center of the frame. Continue to thread beads and pass the string through the remaining holes, until all holes have been threaded and you have created a "web."

Pass the string back through the first hole, letting the end hang approximately 6" from the bottom of the frame. Thread 1–2 beads onto each of the string ends, evening them up, if necessary. Remove tape and tie a feather onto each end.

Dream Catcher

Legend of Spider Woman (Chippewa)

Long ago, humans lived in the sky. The Earth below was dark and covered with water. One day the chief's daughter fell through a hole in the sky. As she fell, the creatures on Earth brought bits of mud from the ocean bottom and covered the back of a turtle shell with it. They built up the mud until it became an island, then a country, then a continent for her to land on.

"The sun lights the sky world," said the chief's daughter, as she sat on the turtle's back.

"I'll go into the sky and bring back the sun," said Raven. But the heat from the sun scorched Raven, turning his beautiful white feathers black.

"I'll try," said Owl. But the sun blistered his eyes, so he can now see only in the dark.

Snake tried, too, but could only wiggle helplessly away from the heat.

Spider Woman watched the other animals try to bring back the sun. Then she wove a silken ladder and climbed into the sky. When she drew near to the sun, she spun a webbed bowl and carried the sun down to Earth in it.

"Thank you Spider Woman," said the animals as they basked in the warm sunlight.

Background Notes: Spider Woman continues to care for the world. Human mothers help Spider Woman by hanging magical webs above their babies' heads. These webs catch bad dreams and let only good dreams filter down the feather into the babies' minds. The circle frame of the dream catcher represents the sun. The web represents Spider Woman's woven house and is usually connected to the hoop at eight points, in honor of Spider Woman's eight legs.

FIVE CIVILIZED TRIBES—WELCOME TO THE SOUTHEAST

Station 4. Shuttlecock Toss

Many Native Americans played a type of game we call "shuttlecock." Sometimes a corncob was tossed into the air. Sometimes cornhusks folded into a square and stuck with feathers were batted with a piece of wood or hands. We'll make shuttlecocks out of fabric and fill them with dried beans to give them weight. Before playing shuttlecock read aloud the WATCH Facts and Notable Natives. At this station you will need:

- These instructions

- Copies of WATCH Facts/Notable Natives to read aloud and hand out

- Copy of *Jump Back* Map of North American Regions with southeast region colored purple

- Purple pencils, crayons, or markers

- 6" square of fabric for each shuttlecock

- 1 heavy rubber band for each shuttlecock

- Dried beans

- 3 stiff feathers for each shuttlecock

- 12" string or yarn for each shuttlecock

- Scissors

Place 1–2 tablespoons of dried beans in the center of the fabric. Gather the ends of cloth and bind them TIGHTLY with the rubber band. Stick the feathers through the top of the rubber band. Wrap and tie string tightly around the rubber band and feather stems. To play, bat the shuttlecock with your hand. See how many times you can hit it into the air without missing.

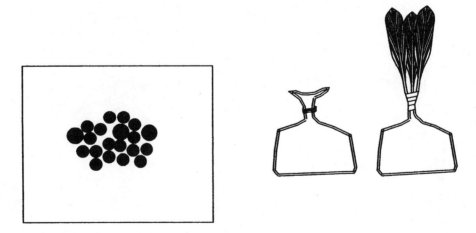

Shuttlecock

TIPS FOR EXTRA FUN

- Using only one hand, try batting the shuttlecock in the air with a heavy paper plate.

- Join in a circle and bat the shuttlecock to the person to your right. Start with one shuttlecock and then try keeping more than one going around the circle.

- Using a box or bucket as a target, stand back and toss your shuttlecock into it. Take one step back every time you hit your target. See how far back you can go.

WATCH Facts (Southeast)

Where: Locate the Southeastern region on the map and color it purple.

Weather: Not too hot or too cold.

What's There: Many forests and plants.

Ate: Hunted deer and other animals by disguising themselves in deerskins to bring deer closer and then shot deer with arrows or darts from blowguns. Hunters might set fire to a forest to flush the deer into a trap. Birds were also hunted. Grew corn, beans, squash, and sunflowers.

Tribes Included: Choctaw, Chickasaw, Seminole, Creek, Cherokee, Caddo, Natchez, Yazoo, Pensacola, Mobile, Alabama, Saponi, Monacan, Eno, Hitchiti, Yamasee, Apalache, Calusa.

Clothing: Deer or other animal skins. Women—wraparound skirt and cape; men—buckskin loincloth (like an apron) and shirt. Barefoot or deerskin moccasins.

Housing: Wooden frames with rough boards plastered with mud and grass; bark roof. To protect against neighboring tribes, villages had tall log fences with watchtowers to shoot from.

Something to think about: In the 1500s, Spanish explorers came into the region killing natives and bringing diseases. They also introduced European culture. When British and French arrived in the 1800s, the Choctaw, Chickasaw, Seminole, Creek, and Cherokee had adopted many white man's customs and became known as the "Five Civilized Tribes."

Notable Natives: Sequoyah's Talking Leaves

Sequoyah (seh-COY-ah), born about 1773, was the son of a Cherokee mother and an English father. He was also known by his English name, George Guess. He never learned to read or write English, but saw that the ability to read and write was a source of power.

Sequoyah wanted to protect the Cherokee culture. He spent 12 years developing over 80 symbols for the Cherokee language. He called his writing system "talking leaves." It allowed Cherokee people to read and write in their own language. In 1824, the Cherokee Council honored him with a medal for his work.

Station 5. Shake, Rattle, and Roll

Rattles and drums are an important part of music and ceremonial dances. People made rattles from turtle shells and gourds (like a hard vegetable squash), filled with small rocks or dried corn. At this station children will make rattles and learn the Cherokee "Legend of Possum". Read the story aloud during or after making the rattles. At this station you will need:

- These instructions
- Copies of "Legend of Possum" to read aloud and hand out
- 1 clean, empty 8 oz. plastic yogurt container with lid for each rattle
- 1 plastic spoon for each rattle
- Colored construction paper
- Dried beans or macaroni
- Duct or strapping tape, scissors, pencil, stapler, colored markers
- Feathers, beads, string, crepe paper for decoration

Cut a strip of paper the height of the container and 1" longer than the circumference (paper can be cut ahead of time). Cut a circle of paper to fit into the indented portion of the lid.

Slice a small slit in the center of the lid and slide the plastic spoon through the slit. Place 1–2 tablespoons of dried beans inside the container and replace the lid. The bowl end of the spoon should be inside the closed container. Tape the lid securely onto the container. Wrap paper strip around the container and secure with a small piece of tape; cut a slit in the paper circle to match the slit in the lid. Slide the circle over the handle and secure it to the lid with 2 overlapped or double-sided pieces of tape.

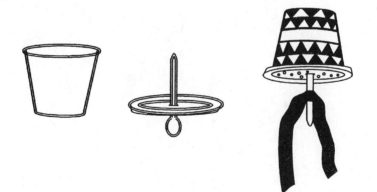

Yo-Gourd Rattle

TIPS FOR EXTRA FUN

- Decorate paper with Native American symbols or designs.
- Wrap handle with paper or add yarn streamers with beads and feathers.
- Rattles will be used at the end-of-the-day dance.

Legend of Possum (Cherokee)

Long ago, Possum had a beautiful, thick tail. Every day he brushed his tail. Every day he combed his tail. Every day he reminded the other animals how beautiful his tail was. When the council meeting was announced, Possum said, "I deserve a seat of honor because of my beautiful tail!"

Rabbit wiggled his nose, remembering how lovely his own tail had been before Bear had pulled it off. "Fine," said Rabbit. "I shall send Cricket to your lodge to comb your tail for you."

Cricket arrived at Possum's lodge. "Everyone at the council meeting is going to love your tail," said Cricket.

Possum smiled and lay down in front of the fire. Soon he was fast asleep. Cricket brushed and wrapped Possum's tail with string. "To keep it neat," Cricket told Possum when he awoke. "When you get to the council meeting," said Cricket, "just remove the string."

Off Possum went. As the other animals settled themselves in their seats, he unwound the string and paraded around the room. But instead of "oooh" and "aaah," all the animals laughed. When Possum turned around he saw why. Cricket had clipped all the hair from his beautiful tail. Now his tail was bald. The lovely fur lay in clumps about the room.

Possum fell to the floor and rolled over, his feet sticking up in the air. And that's what he does even today when he's surprised. Cricket was right. Everyone did love Possum's tail—now that he no longer made such a fuss about it.

Background Notes: Stories were often used to teach lessons. This story probably taught that too much pride was bad. Stories about how animals got their characteristics were common throughout North America. How Rabbit lost his tail is another story!

WHERE THE BUFFALO ROAM—WELCOME TO THE PLAINS

Station 6. Apache Scrolls

Apache people recorded their history on deerskin or buffalo hide. At this station children will use pictures to tell history, a story of their life, or an event in nature. While they are making their Apache scrolls, read aloud WATCH Facts and Notable Natives. You will need:

- These instructions

- Copies of WATCH Facts/Notable Natives to read aloud and hand out

- Copy of *Jump Back* Map of North American Regions with plains region colored yellow

- Yellow pencils, crayons, or markers

- Large brown grocery bag for each scroll

- 2 dowels about 8–12" in length for each scroll

- Masking tape, twine, scissors, ruler, pencil, colored markers, hole punch

Cut open the bag and carefully rip it roughly into an 8" uneven square, to resemble animal hide. Sketch your story on the plain side of the paper. Fill in with colored markers. On the back of the paper, place a piece of masking tape at each of the 4 corners for reinforcement; then punch with a hole punch. Cut four 10" pieces of string and run one through each corner hole. Tie the strings to the tops and bottoms of 2 sticks.

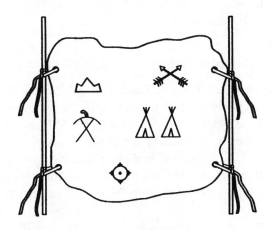

Apache Scroll

TIPS FOR EXTRA FUN

- Pick one funny or important event in your life to display.

- Choose a season or a specific place to recreate in pictures.

- Tell your story to your friends or have them guess what yours means.

WATCH Facts (Plains)

Where: Locate the Plains region and color it yellow.

Weather: Hot and dry in summer; cold in winter.

What's There: Flat, dry grassland—perfect for buffalo to graze.

Ate: Buffalo meat was the main food—roasted, dried into jerky, or mashed with fat and berries into pemmican. People cooperated in several large hunts a year, where buffalo were forced over a cliff, or a ring of fire was set around a herd with an opening where hunters would wait with bows and arrows. After the hunt, buffalo were divided equally among the hunters.

Tribes Included: Some tribes in this area were Cree, Blackfoot, Hidatsa, Crow, Mandan, Sioux, Shoshone, Cheyenne, Pawnee, Oto, Arapaho, Kiowa, Comanche, Wichita, and Apache.

Clothing: Buffalo skin shirts; leggings; knee-length fringed dresses with wide sleeves and flared skirts, decorated with paint or beads; gloves; moccasins. Skins also used as blankets and robes.

Housing: Portable housing (tipis) could be put up or taken down in minutes. To build a tipi, several long poles were tied together at the top. The bottoms were pulled out to make a cone shape and then it was covered in buffalo skins. The tipi floor symbolized the earth. The sides symbolized the sky. The roundness symbolized the circle of life. Groups (Pawnee and Mandan) who lived along water where there were trees built log homes covered with dirt and grass.

Something to think about: In 1800, 60 million buffalo roamed the plains. To keep buffalo off the tracks, railroads hired hunters to kill them, and passengers shot buffalo from the train for fun. By 1900, there were only about 1,000 buffalo left. With few buffalo to eat, many starving Native Americans were forced onto reservations.

Notable Natives: Sitting Bull (Sioux)

The U.S. promised that the Black Hills of Dakota would belong to the Sioux nation forever. But when gold was discovered, miners camped on the land and the U.S. government ordered the Sioux to leave. When the Sioux ignored the order, the U.S. Army prepared to attack.

The Sun Dance is a ceremony performed by many plains people to thank the Great Spirit. Part of the ceremony involved cutting flesh from their bodies as sacrifice. Skewers were poked through their skin and attached to a pole with rawhide. The men danced until their skin ripped free from the skewers. Sometimes the dancers would fall unconscious from the pain. That unconsciousness was seen as supernatural.

Tantanka Iyotake, (a buffalo sitting on his haunches, or "Sitting Bull") was a chief of a major band of the Sioux nation. In 1876, Sitting Bull participated in a Sun Dance ceremony and slashed his arms 100 times in sacrifice. He then had a vision of U.S. soldiers falling in battle. He used this vision to convince the Cheyenne and Arapaho nations to help fight the U.S. Army.

On June 25, 1876, near Little Bighorn River, Montana, Lt. Col. George Armstrong Custer led 225 U.S. Cavalry soldiers into battle. Sitting Bull and his 2,500 warriors quickly defeated them. After the battle, Sitting Bull led his people into Canada but surrendered himself to U.S. troops in 1881. Sitting Bull was known for his fearlessness in battle and for being a kind and wise leader whose deep religious faith gave him special powers to see the future.

Station 7. Buffalo Hunter Training

"Hoop and Pole" was played by many Native American people to practice hunting skills. A hoop made from bent willows was rolled onto a field. Boys and men took turns tossing long poles through the center as they stood or ran along side it. Before playing, read aloud "Legend of the Bluebonnet Flower." At this station you will need:

- These instructions
- Copies of "Legend of the Bluebonnet Flower" to read aloud and hand out
- 2 plastic hula hoops
- 2 thick dowels or broom handles approximately 3' long

Plastic hoops roll best on asphalt surfaces. This game can also be played indoors in a large room. To play "Hoop and Pole" as a relay, divide children into two teams—half of the team at each end of a field. Make the distance long enough to get the hoop rolling and avoid "spearing" each other. On "go" the second person on each team sets the hoop rolling as the first person runs alongside it and tries to spear it with a pole. If the hoop is successfully speared, the player picks it and the pole up and runs to the other side of the field. The player then hands the pole to the first person in line and sets the hoop rolling back in the other direction for that person to spear.

If the hoop falls to the ground before it is speared, the player must return to the front of the line and start over. The relay continues until all people have played. The first team whose players have successfully speared their hoop wins, but allow everyone to have a chance to play.

TIPS FOR EXTRA FUN

- Let each team pick a tribe name (or assign one to them).
- Have the last person in line beat a drum. Everyone chant, "Spear the hoop!"

Legend of the Bluebonnet Flower (Comanche)

Every spring the Comanche people danced and prayed to the creator of the universe. "Oh Great Spirit," they sang, "send us rain and buffalo that we may live and be happy."

One spring the rain did not come. The land turned to dust and the buffalo left. The people were hungry and dying. They sang again to Great Spirit. "Send us rain and buffalo that we may live and be happy."

"You are selfish!" replied Great Spirit. "You have taken from the earth but not given back. Sacrifice something precious. Burn it in fire and offer the ashes to the four winds."

"Surely Great Spirit does not mean for me to sacrifice this buffalo skin I have prepared," said Tall Woman. "I need it to make a new tipi."

"He cannot mean for me to sacrifice my bow," said Brave Man. "I will need it to hunt."

"Great Spirit must want me to have a blanket to keep me warm," said Old Grandfather.

A little girl named She-Who-Is-Alone listened to her people complain. She clutched her cornhusk doll, remembering how her mother had made the doll; remembering how her father had decorated it. After her parents died from hunger, her doll was all she had left of them.

That night while the village slept, She-Who-Is-Alone crept up the hill. There she made a fire and tossed her doll into the flames. When the ashes cooled, she cast them into the four winds. Then she curled up on the ground and cried herself to sleep.

The next morning, She-Who-Is-Alone awoke amid blue flowers, spreading across the plains, turning the land blue as far as she could see. Then as the rain splattered against the dusty earth, she ran singing back to her village.

"Thank you, She-Who-Is-Alone!" shouted the people. "You have sacrificed your precious doll for our sake. We shall call you She-Who-Dearly-Loved-Her-People."

Every year Great Spirit remembers the little girl's sacrifice by covering the land with bluebonnet flowers—a sign that the rains will come again, now and always.

Background Notes: This story shows the connection between the rain, the grass, and the buffalo. Without the rain, the grass dried and the buffalo left. Without the buffalo, the people starved. The bluebonnet, now the state flower of Texas, symbolized the beauty of the spring rains that nourished the grasses, which fed the buffalo and kept the people alive.

PUEBLO PEOPLE—WELCOME TO THE SOUTHWEST

Station 8. Ceremonies in Sand

Navajo medicine men created sand paintings during religious ceremonies. It is believed that these paintings have special powers, especially to heal sick people. The paintings were started early in the morning and destroyed at the end of the ceremony. They were usually made on deerskin or on a level area of sand inside a hogan. Read aloud the WATCH Facts and Notable Natives before or during the sand painting. At this station you will need:

- These instructions
- Copies of WATCH Facts/Notable Natives sheet to read aloud and hand out
- Copy of *Jump Back* Map of North American Regions with southwest region colored red
- Red pencils, crayons, or markers
- Newspapers to cover work area
- Tan poster board
- Dry powdered paint—red, white, yellow, blue, tan
- Paper plates
- Clean sand
- White glue thinned with water (about half and half)
- Paintbrushes, toothpicks, plastic spoons, paper cone spouts, pencils, rulers, craft sticks

This activity can be done outside if it is not too windy. Place the poster board on a covered surface. Draw a design on poster board, using a ruler for straight lines, if needed.

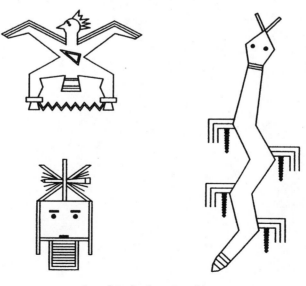

Sand Painting Designs

Put each color of dry paint onto a separate paper plate, add a little sand, and mix. Brush the thinned glue over the penciled design. Sprinkle the dry paint/sand onto the paper. A plastic spoon or a pouring spout made by forming a paper cone will help get colors into small areas. Allow glue to dry slightly and then tap off any loose paint/sand.

TIPS FOR EXTRA FUN

- Sand and paint can be mixed ahead of time.

- Keep the designs large and simple to make it easier to get sand where needed.

- An alternate, simpler activity is to create drawings using crayons on sandpaper.

WATCH Facts (Southwest)

Where: Locate the Southwest region and color it red.

Weather: Little rainfall; hot and cold.

What's There: Mountains, cliffs, canyons, and deserts. Some wild plants, shrubs, grasses, cacti.

Ate: Deer and small animals. Because there was little rain, people dug ditches and dams to get water from rivers for crops (corn, beans, squash, gourds, and tobacco). Wild plants included agave ("mescal" or "century plant"), prickly pear, mesquite pods, and yucca fruit.

Tribes Included: Mojave, Yuma, Pima, Navajo, Hopi, Zuni, Maricopa, Pame, Tiwa, Concho, Papago, Cocopa, Cahita, certain tribes of Apache.

Clothing: Cotton grown as crops. Men—short kilts; women—calf-length blankets wrapped under the left arm and tied at the right shoulder. Sandals made from yucca plant strips.

Housing: Few trees for building. Pueblo people built apartment buildings made of clay or stones and covered with a mixture of mud and grass (called "adobe"). Eastern Apache, who moved here from the Plains, used tipis or built "wikiups" (poles tied together at the top and covered with grass and brush). Navajo built "hogans," five-sided domes covered in clay.

Something to think about: Pueblos didn't have front doors. People climbed a ladder to the top floor and entered a hole in the roof. The ladder was pulled up so enemies couldn't get inside.

Notable Natives: Navajo Code Talkers

Secret communication is important during wartime. Enemies can hear information sent through airwaves on radio and telephones. So armies develop codes for sending information. Enemies work hard to break secret codes. When they do, the information is no longer secret.

During World War II, there was only one U.S. code that was never broken by our enemy. This code was based on the Navajo language, which had no written alphabet. If a person didn't know how to speak Navajo, he would have no way to understand it. The special unit of Navajo Marines who used this code was known as "Navajo Code Talkers."

Part of this secret code used everyday Navajo words for military terms. For example, the word for bird meant a fighter plane. The word for egg meant bombs being dropped from a plane. An "iron fish" was a submarine. The second part of the code strung unrelated words together. The receiver of the message would translate the Navajo words into English. Then the first letters of the translated English words were used to spell English words. For example, the Navajo words "tsah, be-la-sana, ah-keh-di-glini, tsah-ah-dzoh" mean "needle apple victor yucca." That makes no sense. But the first English letters of the translated Navajo words spell out N-A-V-Y.

More than 400 Navajos were trained as code talkers during World War II. Their work saved many American lives. The code was so valuable that it was also used during the Korean and Vietnam wars and was only declassified (made public) by the U.S. government in 1968. In 1972, a Navajo Code Talker exhibit was opened to the public at the Pentagon.

Station 9. Masks and Myths

The Hopi believe spirits, called kachinas (ka-CHI-nas), live on earth for six months and in an underground world for six months. While the kachinas are on earth, they can live inside humans who wear special masks and costumes. Every summer, a 16-day festival is held to honor these spirits and say good-bye as they leave for their underground home. Spirits who controlled the weather were especially helpful. At this station children will make kachina masks. Read the Navajo "Legend of the Five Worlds" before or while making masks. At this station, you will need:

- These instructions

- Copies of "Legend of the Five Worlds" to read aloud and hand out

- 1 sheet of colored construction paper (8½" × 11") for each mask

- 2 lengths of 12" yarn or string each for each mask

- Colored markers, crayons, paper, yarn, feathers, beads, scraps of fabric, crepe paper

- Hole punch, scissors, glue, masking tape

Cut the sheet of paper into any shape—oval, curved, pointed. Cut holes for eyes, nose, and mouth and decorate. Place a strip of tape midway on each side for strength; punch one hole on each side through paper and tape. Thread yarn through the holes and tie mask onto your head.

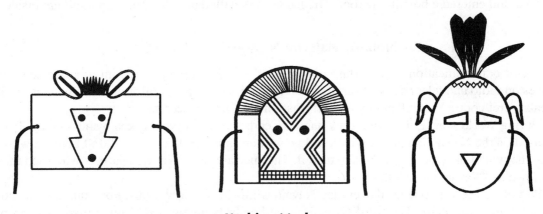

Kachina Masks

TIPS FOR EXTRA FUN

- Decide what spirit your mask will represent. Then decorate it to represent that spirit (bright yellow for sun, blue for sky, splatters or dots for rain, feathers for wind, etc.).

- Masks of trickster kachinas were meant to be funny.

- Masks will be worn at the end-of-the-day dance.

Legend of the Five Worlds (Navajo)

First Man, First Woman, and Coyote lived in the first world—a dark, underground world full of insects and bats. Darkness filled their lives with unhappiness.

"Perhaps it's not so dark in another world," said Coyote as he led First Man, First Woman, and the other creatures upward into a second world.

"Look!" said First Woman. "There are blue birds here!"

"And light from the sun and moon, too," said First Man.

But sometimes darkness still covered the world. So Coyote again led the creatures upward into a third world.

"What wonderful animals live here!" said First Man, pointing to the squirrels and rabbits.

"And other humans!" said First Woman, running to meet the mountain people who also lived in the third world.

"Welcome," said the mountain people. "Enjoy this world, but do not disturb Water Serpent."

Coyote found Water Serpent's children. "What delightful children," said Coyote. Then he kidnapped the children to keep them for his own.

When Water Serpent saw that his children were missing, he hollered. "I shall flood the world until my children return!" As the water rose, the people piled four mountains on top of each other. Then they planted a reed that grew into the sky and climbed it to a fourth world.

But Water Serpent was still angry. "I shall flood the next world, too!" he bellowed.

So again, the people piled the four mountains on top of each other and planted the giant reed. Before they left, they discovered that Coyote had taken Water Serpent's children.

"Send the children back!" they pleaded.

Coyote returned Water Serpent's children and led the people into the fifth world. They huddled on a tiny island in the middle of a huge lake. "Help us, Spirit of Darkness," they prayed.

Spirit of Darkness cut a ditch to drain the water and sent the four winds to dry the soil. And when the land was dry, the people celebrated their life in the new world.

Background Notes: The great ditch cut by Spirit of Darkness is the Colorado River. The fifth world is the world we live in today. Coyote stories are common throughout North America. Coyote is sometimes wise and helpful, sometimes a sneaky trickster. In this story, he is both.

HILLS AND VALLEYS—WELCOME TO THE GREAT BASIN, PLATEAU, AND CALIFORNIA

Station 10. Winning Spinners

Spinners were common toys for many groups of Native Americans. In some places children weren't allowed to play with them after crops were planted. They believed the toy's whizzing sound made the wind blow harder, which would dry out tender plants. Spinners were made with a bone or piece of pottery and animal tendons. Before or while children are making spinners, read aloud the WATCH Facts and Notable Natives. At this station, you will need:

- These instructions

- Copies of WATCH Facts / Notable Natives to read aloud and hand out

- Copy of *Jump Back* Map of North American Regions with the three regions colored blue

- Blue pencils, crayons, or markers

- 2 dowels, approximately 4" long (or 1 chopstick cut in half) for each spinner

- 1 button (2-hole, 1" in diameter or larger with large holes) for each spinner

- 1 length of string 20" long for each spinner thin enough to fit through holes

- Scissors

Double the string in half and tie the folded end to one of the sticks. Thread each loose string end through one buttonhole. Tie ends to the second stick and slide button to the center.

To use the spinner, hold one stick in each hand so that the string is loose enough for the button to hang. Flip the button in a circular motion 6–8 times to wind it up. Pull the twisted string outward to start the button spinning. Relax and pull the string and the button will keep going. Keep relaxing and pulling the string. Listen to the sound of the spinner. Does it sound like the wind?

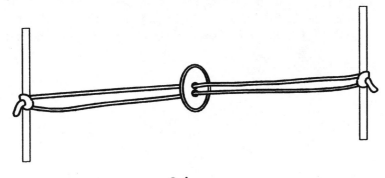

Spinner

TIPS FOR EXTRA FUN

- Draw lines or dots on your button and watch the pattern as it spins.

- Experiment with the direction you wind the spinner and how fast or hard you pull the string. Is there any difference in the sound or speed? Do different buttons make different noises?

WATCH Facts (Great Basin, Plateau, California)

Where: Locate the Great Basin, Plateau, and California regions and color them blue.

Weather: The Great Basin has hot dry summers and cold winters. The Plateau is cold. California is not too hot or cold, with good rainfall.

What's There: Great Basin—little rain so people moved to find water, food, and firewood. Plateau—some forests. California—trees and many animals.

Ate: Great Basin—small animals (rabbits and rodents) in winter, fish year round, birds in spring, wild roots and seeds in spring, rice grass and berries in summer, pine nuts in fall. Plateau—berries, nuts and roots, fish, deer and small game. California—fish, shellfish and sea mammals, deer, small game, and bird; nuts (especially acorns), berries, seeds, roots.

Tribes Included: Great Basin—Bannock, Shoshoni, Paiute, and Gosiute. Plateau—Lake, Columbia, Nez Percé, Spokane, Walla Walla, Klamath, and Modoc. California—Paiute, Shasta, Washoe, Maidu, Ute, Miwok, Mono, Chumash, Yurok, Mohave, Pomo, Yurok, and Yokuts.

Clothing: Great Basin—sagebrush and cedar pounded and woven into shirts and pants for men; blouses and skirts for women. Rabbit skin robes in winter. Plateau—deerskin shirts and leggings. California—hides used as winter clothing; women wore skirts and aprons.

Housing: Great Basin—disposable: circle pole frame covered with reeds. Plateau—winter houses were round log houses built partly underground or wooden lodges covered with mats and earth. Summer houses were bulrush mats over a wooden frame. California—partly underground mounds covered with soil (Maidu), wooden cones covered with brush (Miwok), tree bark planks (Yurok, Hupa, Shasta), or domes covered with tule reed mats (Chumash, Yokuts).

Something to think about: The Chumash had a money system that was used throughout most of California—beads made from different parts of the hard olivella shell.

Notable Natives: Chief Joseph's Military Might

Chief Joseph was born in 1840 in northeastern Oregon. His name, Hin-mah-too-yah-lat-kekt, meant Rolling Thunder Down the Mountain, but he was known as Joseph after his father's baptismal name. When his father died in 1871, Joseph was elected as Chief of the Nez Percé.

Chief Joseph didn't like the U.S. government trying to move his people to a reservation. In 1877, he led a group of about 600 people toward Canada. Along the 1,500 miles, Chief Joseph and his 200 warriors battled nearly 2,000 U.S. soldiers. General William Sherman praised Chief Joseph and his group for their courage and military skill. American newspapers called Chief Joseph "the Red Napoleon," comparing him to the French general, Napoleon Bonaparte.

Throughout his life, Chief Joseph spoke with hope that the American promise of justice and equality would one day extend to his people. In 1904, Chief Joseph died, according to his doctor, of a broken heart.

Station 11. Treetops to Tabletops

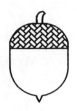

Acorns were a major food in California. After acorns were gathered, they were ground into flour by crushing them on a flat rock or in a rock hole, called a "grinding rock." The flour was washed to remove bitter-tasting acids. Then it was mixed with water and cooked into mush or baked into flat bread. The board game Treetops to Tabletops is a fun way to learn about acorns. Native Americans in this region didn't use tables, but you get the idea. Read aloud the legend "How Coyote Made Man" before playing the game. At this station you will need:

- These instructions

- Copies of "How Coyote Made Man" to read aloud and hand out

- One copy of Treetops to Tabletops game board for every two children (enlarge as needed on the copying machine)

- One game piece for each child

- One die per game board

Each player rolls the die—the highest number plays first. Roll the die and move the game piece along the board the number of spaces shown on the die. Follow the instructions on each space—reading aloud what is written on the space. The first one to the dinner table wins!

TIPS FOR EXTRA FUN

- Game boards can be laminated and reused or each child can have a game as a souvenir.

- Place a dot of different colors on acorns to use as game pieces.

- If acorns are not available, use dried beans, nuts in shells, or other small items.

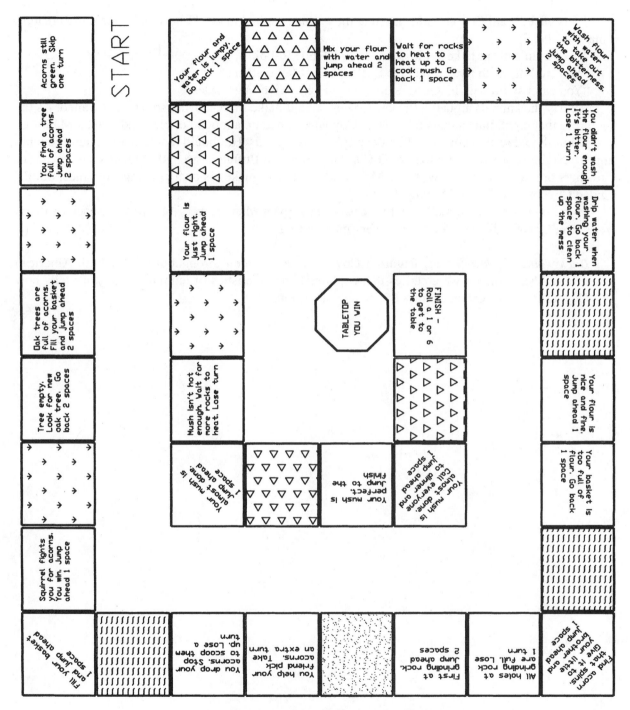

Treetops to Tabletops Board Game

START

Acorns still green. Skip one turn

You find a tree full of acorns. Jump ahead 2 spaces

Oak trees are full of acorns. Fill your basket and jump ahead 2 spaces

Tree empty. Look for new oak tree. Go back 2 spaces

Squirrel fights you for acorns. You win. Jump ahead 1 space

Fill your basket and jump ahead 1 space

You drop your acorns. Stop to scoop them up. Lose a turn

You help your friend pick acorns. Take an extra turn

First at grinding rock. Jump ahead 2 spaces

All holes at grinding rock are full. Lose 1 turn

Find acorn that little brother and give it to your spins. Jump ahead 1 space

Your flour and water is lumpy. Go back 1 space

Mix your flour with water and jump ahead 2 spaces

Wait for rocks to heat to heat up to cook mush. Go back 1 space

Wash flour with water to take out the bitterness. Jump ahead 2 spaces

You didn't wash the flour enough washing your flour. It's bitter. Lose 1 turn

Drip water when flour. Go back 1 space to clean up the mess

Your flour is nice and fine. Jump ahead 1 space

Your basket is too full of flour. Go back 1 space

Your flour is just right. Jump ahead 1 space

Mush isn't hot enough. Wait for more rocks to heat. Lose turn

Your mush is almost done. Jump ahead 1 space

Your mush is almost perfect. Jump to the finish

Your mush is almost done. Call everyone to dinner and jump ahead 1 space

FINISH – Roll a 1 or 6 to get to the table

TABLETOP YOU WIN

How Coyote Made Man (Maidu, Yurok, and other tribes)

"Very nice!" said Coyote as he gazed at the animals he had made. "I have only one more creature to make—Man."

"Give Man soft fur to keep him warm," said gentle Rabbit.

"You can't fly with fur," said brave Eagle. "Give Man feathers."

"You can't swim with feathers," said speedy Fish. "Give Man scales."

All day the animals argued over how Coyote should make Man. Coyote smiled and waited. As the moon rose that night, the animals fell asleep. Coyote scooped up a mound of clay and shaped Man.

"Man should walk on two legs like Bear," Coyote decided. "He should roar like Mountain Lion, but sing like Nightingale. Man should have Owl's sharp eyes and Buffalo's strength. Man does not need fur or feathers or scales, because I will give Man hands so he can make his own clothing. And most of all," decided Coyote, "I will give Man my wisdom."

In the morning, the animals saw that Coyote had given Man the very best parts of each of them. "Very nice, Coyote," they said together. "Very nice, indeed."

Background Notes: Stories featuring Coyote were common throughout many North American tribes. Also common were stories that explained characteristics of animals. This story tells how Coyote chose the characteristics of one animal—Man.

TOTEMS AND TALES—WELCOME TO THE NORTHWEST COAST

Station 12. Blanket Weavers

Chilkat blankets are five-sided fringed capes made from mountain goat fur and cedar bark and worn during ceremonies, dances, and potlatch feasts. The designs are identical on both halves of the blanket and represent clan symbols, humans, or animals. When the blanket is worn while dancing, the arms are spread out to show off the design. Before or while making Chilkat blankets, read aloud the WATCH Facts and Notable Natives. At this station you will need:

- These instructions
- Copies of WATCH Facts/Notable Natives to read aloud and hand out
- Copy of *Jump Back* Map of North American Regions with northwest region colored orange
- Orange pencils, crayons, or markers and other assorted colors
- 1 brown paper grocery bag for each blanket
- Copy of Sample Chilkat Blanket Designs for inspiration
- 2 lengths of yarn or string 6–8" long for each blanket
- Hole punch, scissors, pencils, masking tape

Cut brown paper bag open at the back seam, remove bottom, and spread open lengthwise, with plain side facing up. Cut bottom corners at a 45-degree angle so the bag is now five-sided. Fold bag in half widthwise to mark the center point, then reopen. Outline large designs with heavy black marker and copy the design from one half of the bag to the other so that both sides are identical. Fill in designs with colored markers. Allow an undecorated border around the four lower sides. Snip approximately 4" deep fringe around the lower four sides, leaving the top edge uncut. Place strip of masking tape at two top corners to strengthen and punch a hole at each edge. Attach string, drape over shoulders, and tie.

TIPS FOR EXTRA FUN

- Before cutting fringe, crumple the paper to give it an "old" look.
- Make designs that represent something important in your life such as a pet or a hobby.
- Discuss making yarn out of tree bark—how to strip bark off trees, softening bark by soaking it in water, splinters!

Face

Bear's paws

Bird's Feet

Eyes or
socket joints

Whale

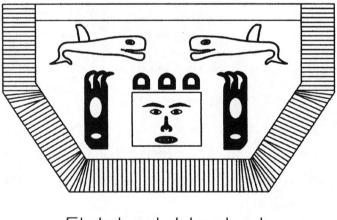

Finished blanket

Sample Chilkat Blanket Designs

WATCH Facts (Northwest)

Where: Locate the Northwest region and color it orange.

Weather: Rainy but mild.

What's There: Forests, rivers, mountains.

Ate: Wild berries, roots, seaweed, sea mammals, shellfish, deer, goats, bears, small animals, salmon—people spent six months catching and drying fish to eat the rest of the year, giving them six months for art, trade, and ceremonies, such as the potlatch (POT-lach), a multiday feast, where the host gave gifts to prove his rank and wealth.

Tribes Included: Tlingit, Haida, Bella Bella, Nootka, Skokomish, Chimakum, Duwamish, Suquamish, Chinook, Clatsop, Tillamook, Coos, Kwakiutl, and Tsimshiam.

Clothing: Goat wool mixed with cedar bark blankets and clothes. Women wore fringed skirts or leather dresses. Men wore leather breechcloths (aprons) except in cold, wet weather when they wore leather shirts and leggings. Everyone wore woven hats in rainy weather.

Housing: A 30–35' "lodge" made from wooden boards housed several families. Carved totem poles stood at the front of an important person's house telling that person's family history.

Something to think about: The Tlingit people caught eulachon fish, called "candlefish." They dried this oily fish and burned them like candles. Imagine if you had candlefish on your birthday cake. What would you wish for?

Notable Natives: Chief Seattle

Chief Seattle was born in Washington State about 1875. He was the son of a Suquamish chief and a Duwamish woman. The position of Suquamish Chief was gained through courage in battle. Seattle was chief of both the Suquamish and Duwamish tribes.

In 1854, the U.S. government tried to move the Suquamish and Duwamish tribes to a reservation. Chief Seattle is famous for a speech he made at a treaty ceremony in 1854. The city of Seattle, Washington, was later named after him. Chief Seattle died on June 7, 1866. The letters I.H.S. on his tombstone stand for the Latin phrase, "in hoc spiritus," which means, "I have suffered."

Station 13. Fun with Frontlets

At this station, children make frontlets and hear the legend "How Raven Stole the Heavens." Frontlets are wooden headdresses worn by nobles on the northwestern coast, carved and painted with human and animal figures. Frontlets were worn at important ceremonies and were sometimes decorated with feathers, sea lion whiskers, leather, or fur. Read aloud the legend during or after making the frontlets. At this station you will need:

- These instructions

- Copies of "How Raven Stole the Heavens" to read aloud and hand out

- 1 brown paper grocery bag for each frontlet

- Colored markers, scissors, stapler, glue, tape

Cut along the back seam of a brown paper grocery bag, cut off the bottom, and lie it flat, printed side up. Fold the bag in half lengthwise, so the printed side is now inside. Wrap the paper around your head and mark to fit. Cut the paper about 2" longer than your mark.

Even out the top cut edges of your paper. Decorate with an animal or human face on the front and outline with black markers. Staple the ends together to form your headdress.

Frontlet

TIPS FOR EXTRA FUN

- Tape or staple feathers or straw to the sides or front of the headdress so that they stick up or make paper "fringe" by cutting a few inches down from the top.

- These frontlets can be worn at the end-of-the-day dance instead of the kachina masks.

- Have everyone share their designs and why they chose them.

How Raven Stole the Heavens (Tlingit, Haida, Kwakiutl, and Tsimshiam)

When the world was new, Raven listened to the people shuffle through the darkness. "I must help the people," said Raven. He flew east to the lodge of the Chief of Heaven. Raven rested on a branch of a pine tree and watched the chief's daughter, Spirit Maiden, kneel by a stream. He turned himself into a pinecone seed and dropped into Spirit Maiden's cupped hands. As she sipped cool water, she swallowed the tiny seed.

In time, a child was born to Spirit Maiden. The child had sharp, black eyes and sleek black hair. Its cries were quick, like the cawing of a bird. Spirit Maiden loved her child. But her father, Chief of Heaven, loved him more.

Chief of Heaven carried the child everywhere, laughing and bouncing the baby who filled his life with joy. One day, the black-haired child began to cry, pointing to a carved wooden box that stood in a corner of the chief's great lodge.

"Why are you crying, dear boy?" asked Chief of Heaven, handing him a carved toy.

The child tossed the toy onto the floor, pointed to the box, and cried harder.

"Are you thirsty?" said Chief of Heaven, offering him water from a tightly woven basket.

The child pushed the basket away, pointed to the box, and cried harder.

"Surely you are hungry," said Chief of Heaven, handing him a sliver of dried salmon.

The child tossed the salmon to the floor, pointed to the box, and cried harder.

Chief of Heaven set the carved box in front of the child. The child smiled and before Chief of Heaven could stop him, the child opened it.

Poof! A million stars flew out of the box, up through the smoke hole, and into the sky.

Poof! A silver moon flew out of the box, up through the smoke hole, and into the sky.

Poof! A flaming sun flew out of the box, up through the smoke hole, and into the sky.

And before Chief of Heaven could understand what happened, his dear, black haired grandchild became a raven, flew through the smoke hole, and was gone. That is why a million stars, a silver moon, and a flaming sun brighten our world today.

Background Notes: The northwest coast tribes have many stories about Raven and his adventures. Just like the Coyote stories, Raven is sometimes a hero and sometimes a trickster. In this story, Raven uses his special powers and trickery to help humans.

MUKLUK MANIA—WELCOME TO THE SUBARCTIC AND ARCTIC

Station 14. Bundles of Sticks

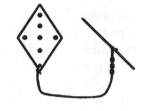

Stick games were common among many Native Americans. Each group of 3 or 4 children should have one game set between them. Before playing, read aloud the WATCH Facts and Notable Natives. At this station you will need:

- These instructions

- Copies of WATCH Facts/Notable Natives to read aloud and hand out

- Copy of *Jump Back* Map of North American Regions with regions colored brown

- Brown pencils, crayons, or markers

- 10 bamboo skewers or "pick-up sticks" per game

- Pencils and paper

To play the game, decide who plays first alphabetically by first name. The first person holds the sticks in a bundle and releases them so they fall into a pile. Score one point for each stick that crosses another stick and mark that number down under the player's name. The next player repeats the process until all have played. The first person to reach 30 points wins.

TIPS FOR EXTRA FUN

- Use a separating stick to take away a stick without moving any others. Continue your turn until you move a stick that you are not intending to remove. It is then the next person's turn. The player with the most sticks after one round wins.

- One person holds the sticks in a bundle but secretly removes some number of sticks. The other players have to guess how many are left.

- Colored, store bought "pick-up sticks" can be used for these games.

WATCH Facts (Subarctic/Arctic)

Where: Locate subarctic and arctic areas and color them brown.

Weather: Brutally cold.

What's There: Rough coastlines, rushing rivers, and tundra (plains with few plants except moss, lichen, and bushes). Too cold for trees to grow. Most of the year the land is covered in ice and snow. During the short, cold summer, the tundra thaws at the surface but water can't drain away through the permanently frozen soil underneath and the land becomes a soggy marsh.

Ate: Seal in winter. The ocean freezes, so people first find air holes made by seals scratching through the ice to breathe. Smaller foxes, squirrels, birds, fish in spring. Seals, walrus, whales, or caribou (a deer-like animal), birds, and rabbits on the tundra in early summer.

Tribes Included: Hare, Athabasca, Yup'ik, Inupiaq, Aleut. Arctic people called themselves "Inuit," which means "the people." Other tribes called them "Eskimos," which means "raw flesh eaters." Since there are few trees to burn as fuel for cooking, meat was often eaten raw.

Clothing: Men and women in the south wore slip-on dresses with long sleeves and attached hoods, leather moccasins, caribou-skin boots or snowshoes; caribou or rabbit skin robe in winter. Arctic clothing was seal or caribou skin boots (mukluks), mittens, pants, and parkas.

Housing: Houses partly underground covered in sod (grass with soil attached) or wigwams (covered with caribou skins). Arctic houses were igloos, built from packed snow blocks.

Something to think about: What do you drink if the only water around is in the salty ocean? Surprise! Very old sea ice loses its salt. So Inuits melted old sea ice for drinking water.

Notable Natives: Maniilaq, The Prophet (Inuit)

Maniilaq was born in the early 1800s near the southern slopes of Brooks Mountain, along the Upper Kobuk River. He died about 1890. He heard what he called a "source of knowledge" and made predictions.

Many of Maniilaq's predictions have come true. He predicted that boats powered by fire would travel in water (motorboats) and in the sky (airplanes). He said that thin bark would be used to write on (paper). He also said that people with light skin and light hair would arrive in the arctic world and that the Inuit lifestyle would change forever. Maniilaq is remembered as a teacher of kindness and faith in God. He helped his people work through fears by using reason rather than relying on magic.

Station 15. Igloos and Icicles

Ring and pin games were common throughout North America. Inuits made their game from seal bones and tendons, sometimes adding fish backbones to weight the ring. In another form of this game, a target was hung from the ceiling of the igloo and everyone tried to spear the wiggly target at once. Smart players wore thick mittens to avoid being stabbed! Read aloud "Legend of Sedna, Maiden of the Sea" before or while making the game. At this station you will need:

- These instructions

- Copies of "Legend of Sedna, Maiden of the Sea" to read aloud and hand out

- 1 bamboo skewer, cut to 6" long for each game (keep pointed end) or long nail

- Length of string approximately 18" long for each game

- 5–6 colored beads for each game

- Poster board approximately 6" × 4" for each game

- Copies of Ring and Pin pattern

- Pencil, scissors, hole punch

Trace the pattern onto poster board and cut out. (Save time by cutting targets ahead of time with a paper cutter.) Punch holes where indicated. Tie one end of the string to the end hole of the target. Thread several beads onto the string and tie to the middle of the skewer (or nail). To play, hold skewer pointed end up. Swing target and try to catch it with the skewer.

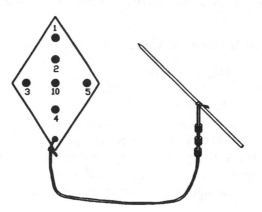

Ring and Pin Game

TIPS FOR EXTRA FUN

- Use colored poster board or decorate target with markers.

- Assign point numbers to the holes and keep score. The first to reach 20 wins.

- Try to catch the ring in numbered order: first catch the number 1 hole, then the number 2 hole, etc.

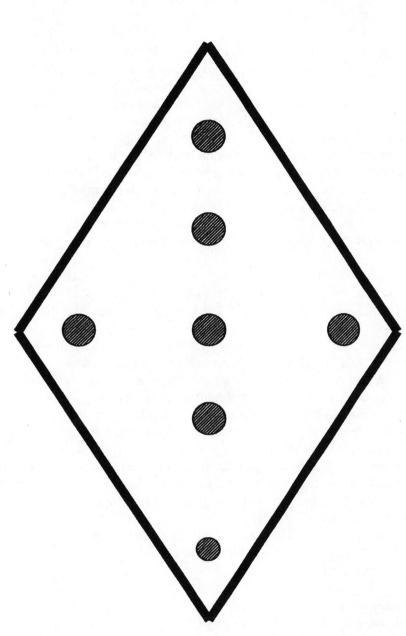

Ring and Pin Pattern

Legend of Sedna, Maiden of the Sea (Inuit)

"No!" shouted Sedna, stomping her mukluk-booted foot. "I won't marry any of them!"

"A young hunter will provide food," Sedna's father scolded. "You will marry the next man who asks you!"

The next man spoke through hand signals, his face hidden in the shadows of his fur-trimmed hood. Sedna's father agreed to the marriage and the man took Sedna in his kayak to a distant island. When he removed his parka, Sedna saw he was not a man—but a sea bird!

"How foolish I was," cried Sedna, "not to have married one of the fine young hunters."

All through the fierce winter, the chilly spring, and the marshy summer, Sedna cried. She had no sod hut; not even an igloo to keep out the bitter wind. Sharp rocks were her bed on the sea bird's cliff. Sedna's sobs were carried by the harsh autumn winds back to her father's hut.

"What have I done?" asked Sedna's father, hearing her moans. He jumped into his kayak and followed Sedna's cries, reaching the rocky shore as the winter winds began to blow.

"Father!" Sedna cried, running to him. "I was so foolish!"

"Daughter!" her father cried. "I'm sorry I sent you to such a cruel fate."

"We must go quickly," said Sedna. "while my husband is fishing." They climbed into the kayak and paddled out to sea.

The sea bird was furious when he returned and set out to find Sedna. He beat his wings to make the wind whip over the ocean. The waves slapped against the tiny kayak.

"My husband will not stop until I return," screamed Sedna, clutching the tipping boat. "We will both die!"

"Hide beneath the water," shouted her father. "He will think you have drowned."

Sedna slipped under the freezing water as her husband circled overhead.

"Aaargh!" Sedna gasped, coming up for air. She tried to grip the boat, but her fingertips, now frozen to the first joint, cracked and fell off, becoming seals as they dropped into the water.

Again Sedna's sea bird husband circled overhead. Again Sedna hid under the freezing water. When she returned to the surface to clutch the boat, the ends of her frozen fingers broke at the second joint, becoming walruses as they fell into the water.

A third time Sedna's sea bird husband circled overhead and a third time Sedna hid under the freezing water. When she returned to the surface, her frozen fingers broke at the last joint—this time becoming whales as they fell into the water. And with no fingers to grip the boat, Sedna called out, "Forgive me, Father!" and slid into the icy water forever.

There Sedna lives still, ruling the ocean and the creatures in it. Although Sedna learned a lesson, even today her pride and anger sometimes get the better of her. When that happens, it is best to stay far away from the roaring ocean waves.

Background Notes: The Inuits believe that since Sedna has no fingers, she can no longer brush her long hair. Shaman (religious leaders) sometimes dive underwater and offer to brush her hair so she will be happy and the seas will be calm.

END THE DAY AS A GROUP

Station 16. Pow Wow Wow Dance

Children come together at the end of the day for a multicultural dance. They wear their kachina masks or frontlets, use their rattles, and learn dance steps. Alternate playing drums while others perform. At this station, you will need:

- Dance step and rhythm instructions

- Drums or empty boxes

- Each child's kachina masks, frontlets, and rattles

DANCE STEPS AND RHYTHMS

Toe-Heel Step: Drumbeat is ONE-two (LOUD-soft). On ONE, touch ground with left toe; on TWO, bring left heel down hard. Repeat with right foot. Go in a circle, backward, or side-to-side.

Drag Step: Drumbeat is one-TWO (soft-LOUD). Touch toe to ground on one. On TWO, drag foot backward stomping heel.

Canoe Step: Drumbeat is ONE-two-three-four (LOUD-soft-soft-soft). On ONE, step on left foot. Tap right foot on two-three-four. Then step forward with right foot on ONE and tap left foot on two-three-four. Swing arms like you're rowing a canoe—first on one side of the body, then the other.

TIPS FOR EXTRA FUN

- Sprinkle cornmeal on the ground as a prayer for rain, growth, and abundance.

- Pueblo people had clown kachinas in their dances, so have fun!

Station 17. Potlatch

Take group photos and assemble souvenir booklets while snacking on some of the following (provide paper plates, cups, napkins, utensils as needed):

- Fresh berries or fruit

- Nuts, pumpkin or sunflower seeds, popcorn

- Tamales (Chumash) or tortillas (similar to piki bread)

- Jerky or pemmican

TIPS FOR EXTRA FUN

- Switch this station to midday for a lunchtime feast.

- Instead of a stapled souvenir booklet, make parfleches at this station.

- Have children wear and carry items they have made for the group photograph.

- SMILE!

Chapter 4

Colonial America Day

Welcome to Colonial America Day. During this day of fun, children will rotate through stations sampling life in Colonial America. They will start the day as a single group, participating in organizational activities to gear them up for learning. Then they will split into smaller groups, rotate through stations, and join up again at the end of the day with activities to summarize what they've learned. The stations and activities for Colonial America Day are:

Start the Day as a Group

Station 1. Just off the Boat (Pin the Colony on the Map, gathering bag, songs, and F.U.N. Facts—Delaware. Children split into groups and proceed to stations)

Colonial Home Life

Station 2. What's the Buzz? It's a Quilting Bee! (F.U.N. Facts—Pennsylvania; Paper Quilts)

Station 3. This-Little-Light-of-Mine Candle Making (F.U.N. Facts—New Jersey; Homemade Candle)

Station 4. Firkin, Pottle, Pinch, and Sack (F.U.N. Facts—Georgia; Measurements)

Colonial Business and School Life

Station 5. Fine Feathered Pens (F.U.N. Facts—Connecticut; Quill Pens)

Station 6. Tinkering with Tin (F.U.N. Facts—Massachusetts; Tin Art)

Station 7. Honk, Honk? No, Moo! (F.U.N. Facts—Maryland; Hornbooks)

Colonial Living

Station 8. What Time Is It? Check Your Sundial (F.U.N. Facts—South Carolina; Sundial)

Station 9. The Rooster Says a Storm Is Coming (F.U.N. Facts—New Hampshire; Weathervanes)

Station 10. Curly Qs (F.U.N. Facts—Virginia; Quilling)

Colonial Fun and Games

Station 11. Jolly Jumpers (F.U.N. Facts—New York; Puppets)

Station 12. Nine Men's Morris (F.U.N. Facts—North Carolina; Board Game)

Station 13. Top It Off! (F.U.N. Facts—Rhode Island; Tops)

End the Day as a Group

Station 14. Quick Quoits

Station 15. Nine Pin

Station 16. Thanksgiving Fun (Feast, Photos, Booklets)

NAMETAGS

Use the following for group nametags or think up your own:

Powhatans	Hornbook Holders	South Carolinians
Pilgrims	Delawareans	New Hampshirites
May Flowers	Pennsylvanians	Virginians
Colonialists	New Jersey-ites	New Yorkers
Captain Smith's Crew	Georgians	North Carolinians
Yankee Doodles	Connecti-cutters	Rhode Islanders
Penn's Friends	Massachusetts-ites	
Wig Wearers	Mary Landers	

COSTUME IDEAS

Kids and adults will have more fun if they dress in costume. Boys wore knee-length pants, vests, and jackets. Girls always wore hats (usually bonnets), even at home. Dresses were always floor length with full skirts. Girls also wore "wings," a triangle cloth worn over shoulders like a shawl. When working at home, girls wore aprons to protect their dresses. Dutch farm women wore a heavy brass chain around their waists called a chatelaine (SHA-ti-lane). Keys, scissors, and sewing tools hung from it. Everyone wore cloaks. Cloth was wool until cotton was grown in the southern colonies. Quaker people wore no colors except gray and brown. Remember that many European cultures as well as Native Americans can be represented in colonial costumes.

Men wore "sherry vallies" and "spatter dashs" (leggings) to protect pants and shoes from mud. Girls wore platform shoes called "pattens" or "goloe-shoes," a thick piece of wood strapped to shoes to lift them above the mud. Our old-fashioned word for boots, "galoshes," comes from the term "goloe-shoes." Have a piece of wood handy to try strapping to shoes.

START THE DAY AS A GROUP

Station 1. Just off the Boat

Children assemble at this station, make their gathering bags (see Chapter 1) and sing songs. Using the *Jump Back* Map of Colonial America as a guide, play Pin the Colony on the Map—locating the colonies on a map and marking them with sticky notes. Children are then organized into rotation groups and given their nametags and the first F.U.N. Facts (Delaware). F.U.N. Facts can be read aloud at each station and placed in gathering bags for the end of the day. Children locate Delaware on their *Jump Back* Map of Colonial America and color it red. For this station you will need:

- These instructions
- A large U.S. map
- Copy of *Jump Back* Map of Colonial America for each child
- Sticky notes with names of colonies, plus one labeled "Spanish Territories," and one labeled "French Territories"
- Red pencils, crayons, or markers
- Items to make gathering bags (see Chapter 1)
- Copy of song sheets or one of each song for overhead projector or leader
- Copy of F.U.N. Facts—Delaware for each child

TIPS FOR EXTRA FUN

- Background music adds interest. Try the public library for music and use a tape or CD player with extension cords, if needed. A piano or guitar is fun or kids can take turns accompanying music with boxes, pans, and sticks.
- Ask children who have dressed in costume to explain what culture they represent.
- Provide costumes or accessories at the first station for kids to try on or wear throughout the day or provide costumes at certain stations to wear only at that station.

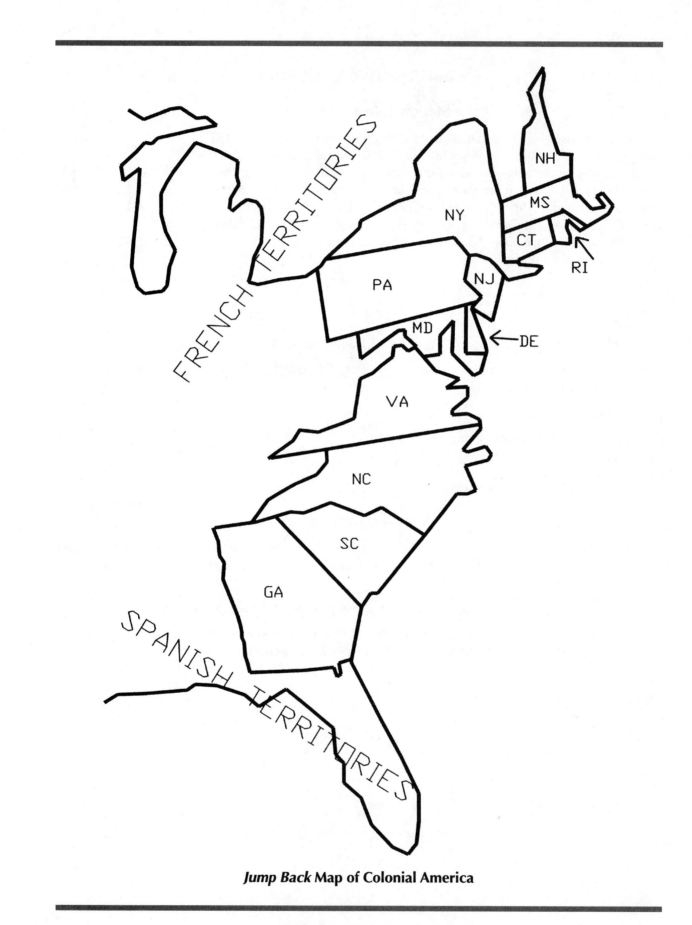

Jump Back Map of Colonial America

Yankee Doodle

Yankee Doodle went to town
A-riding on a pony,
Stuck a feather in his hat
And called it macaroni.

Chorus: Yankee Doodle, keep it up!
Yankee Doodle dandy,
Mind the music and the step,
And with the girls be handy.

Verse 2: Father and I went down to camp
Along with Captain Gooding,
And there we saw the men and boys
As thick as hasty pudding.

Chorus

Verse 3: There was Captain Washington
Upon a slapping stallion,
A-giving orders to his men;
I guess there was a million.

Chorus

Background Notes: The American colonialists who fought alongside British troops during the French and Indian Wars looked tattered in their buckskins and furs next to the polished British uniforms. This song was meant to make fun of those colonial troops. Instead, the colonialists took up the song with pride. But why did Yankee Doodle stick pasta in his hat? Back then "macaroni" didn't refer to pasta. "Macaroni" was a fancy style of Italian clothes. By sticking a feather in his cap and calling himself a fancy dresser, Yankee Doodle was saying he was proud to be a country bumpkin.

Billy Boy

Oh, where have you been, Billy Boy, Billy Boy?
Oh, where have you been, charming Billy?
I have been to seek a wife,
She's the darling of my life.
She's a young thing and cannot leave her mother.

Did she bid you to come in, Billy Boy, Billy Boy?
Did she bid you to come in, charming Billy?
Yes, she bade me to come in,
There's a dimple on her chin,
She's a young thing and cannot leave her mother.

Can she bake a cherry pie, Billy Boy, Billy Boy?
Can she bake a cherry pie, charming Billy?
She can bake a cherry pie
In the twinkling of an eye.
She's a young thing and cannot leave her mother.

How old is she, Billy Boy, Billy Boy?
How old is she, charming Billy?
She's three times six, four times seven,
Twenty-eight and eleven.
She's a young thing and cannot leave her mother.

Background Notes: Like many of the songs in Colonial America, this song may have been brought over from England. It is not known who wrote the words or the music.

On Top of Old Smoky

On top of Old Smoky, all covered with snow,
I lost my true lover for courting too slow.
Now courting is pleasure, but parting is grief,
And a false-hearted lover is worse than a thief.

    A thief will just rob you and take what you have,
    But a false-hearted lover will lead you to the grave.
    The grave will decay you and turn you to dust.
    Not one boy in a hundred a poor girl can trust.

They'll hug you and kiss you and tell you more lies
Than the crossties on the railroad or the stars in the skies.
Come all you young maidens and listen to me:
Never place your affection on a green willow tree.

    The leaves they will wither, the roots they will die.
    You'll all be forsaken and never know why.
    On top of Old Smoky, all covered with snow,
    I lost my true lover for courting too slow.

Background Notes: "Old Smoky" is the name of a mountain in the Great Smoky Mountain Range, located partly in North Carolina and partly in present-day Tennessee.

F.U.N. FACTS—Delaware

Famous People: The colony of Delaware was started by Dutch fur traders, then became a Swedish settlement, and returned to Dutch ownership before the English took it after winning a war in Europe. It was renamed after **Lord de la Warr,** the British lord who brought supplies and settlers to America after the English settled Jamestown, Virginia.

Unusual Tidbit: Everyone in colonial times wore dresses until the age of five— even boys. Sometimes, those lacy dresses made it hard to tell the baby boys from the baby girls!

Number: 1—Delaware was the first colony to become a state. Locate Delaware on your *Jump Back* Map of Colonial America and color it red.

COLONIAL HOME LIFE

Station 2. What's the Buzz? It's a Quilting Bee!

Colonial settlers couldn't go to the department store to buy what they needed. They had to make many things at home from whatever they had. New blankets (quilts) were sewn together using pieces of old clothes or left-over scraps. Sometimes many people would get together and have a party called a "quilting bee." Everyone would work together to make one quilt. Because different pieces of cloth were used, many quilts had colorful designs and patterns.

Today we'll make a paper quilt mural for our end-of-the-day photographs. Using the *Jump Back* Quilt Patterns for inspiration, children will make their own quilt block using colored paper and glue and place it on a larger sheet of butcher paper for a mural. Before or while making quilt patterns, read aloud the F.U.N. Facts—Pennsylvania, locate the colony on the *Jump Back* Map, and color it yellow. For this station you will need:

- These instructions
- Base paper for mural (either butcher paper, poster board, or individual sheets of paper)
- Colored construction paper
- Scissors
- Glue
- *Jump Back* Quilt Patterns for ideas
- Copy of F.U.N. Facts—Pennsylvania for each child
- Yellow pencils, crayons, or markers

TIPS FOR EXTRA FUN

- Instead of one giant quilt mural, have each rotating group create a poster board mural.
- Instead of one quilt mural, each child can create a single 11" × 18" quilt composed of smaller quilt blocks.
- Precut colored squares, diamonds, and triangles to save time.
- Lead a discussion about colonial recycling. What other things could scraps of fabric be used for? (Braided "rag rugs," children's clothing made from adult clothes, sacks and pouches, sweaters unraveled and re-knit)

4 IN A BLOCK

AUNT ELIZA'S STAR

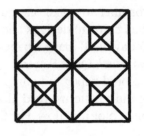

GRANDMOTHER'S OWN

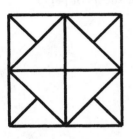

RIGHT AND LEFT

MOTHER'S DREAM

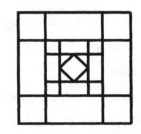

DIAMOND IN A SQUARE

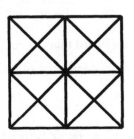

JUMP BACK 1

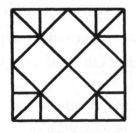

JUMP BACK 2

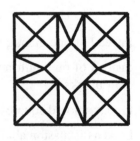

JUMP BACK 3

Jump Back **Quilt Patterns**

F.U.N. FACTS—Pennsylvania

Famous People: William Penn was a member of the Society of Friends (Quaker) religion. King Charles II gave land to Penn in payment of a debt the King owed to Penn's father. In England, all religions except the Church of England were against the law. William Penn founded the colony of Pennsylvania so Quakers could practice their religion.

Unusual Tidbit: Many colonial families had chickens that provided eggs and meat for food and feathers for pillows and mattresses. The chickens also had an important cleaning task. Colonialists would toss a live chicken down the chimney. The chicken would squawk and flap its wings all the way down—sweeping the soot from the inside of the chimney as it went!

Number: 2—Pennsylvania was the second colony to become a state. Locate Pennsylvania on your *Jump Back* Map of Colonial America and color it yellow.

Station 3. This-Little-Light-of-Mine Candle Making

Because electricity had not been invented yet, colonial people used candles for light. Where did they get candles? They made them at home. The fat (tallow—TAL-low) from raw meat was saved until there was enough to make candles. Then a string, called a wick, was dipped over and over in hot fat until layers of fat thickened enough to make a candle. The fat-covered strings were hung to dry and harden into candles. Today we'll make homemade candles with paraffin (wax). Let's see how long it will take to make a candle thick enough to light our homes. While making candles, read aloud the F.U.N. Facts—New Jersey, locate the colony on the *Jump Back* Map of Colonial America, and color it purple. Consider having two adults at this station. For this station you will need:

- These instructions
- Wicks—precut to approximately 8" lengths—enough for one for each child
- Paraffin—allow enough to fill a coffee can adequately for dipping; allow one can for every 3–4 children in the group
- Camp stove for heating and reheating paraffin
- Camp stove fuel and lighter
- Newspaper to cover work area
- Piece of wood to place under each coffee can
- Potholders or oven mitts
- Copy of F.U.N. Facts—New Jersey for each child
- Purple pencils, crayons, or markers

Heat paraffin ahead of time and reheat as needed during the day. Children continue to dip their wicks into the wax for the duration of the station timing. Candles will be quite thin by the end of the station, illustrating the time and effort colonists put into making candles.

TIPS FOR EXTRA FUN

- Add coloring or scent to paraffin.
- During dipping, discuss: How long would it take to make a 1" diameter candle? If colonialists used one candle a night, how long would it take to make enough candles for a week? A month? A year? How many candles would a family use per week? Per month? Per year?
- Discuss gadgets to dip more than one candle at a time, use of molds, the smell of animal fat versus scented candles we use today.

F.U.N. FACTS—New Jersey

Famous People: King Charles II granted the land that became New Jersey to **Sir George Carteret** and **Lord Berkeley**. The area later became a colony and was named "New Jersey" in honor of Sir Carteret, the governor of the Isle of Jersey in England.

Unusual Tidbit: Colonial men and women (and sometimes children) wore wigs. Some wigs were made from human hair, but even wigs made from animal hair were expensive. People had to pay attention or thieves would snatch their hairdos right off their heads.

Number: 3—New Jersey was the third colony to become a state. Locate New Jersey on your *Jump Back* Map of Colonial America and color it purple.

Station 4. Firkin, Pottle, Pinch, and Sack

Colonial school kids learned the "three Rs"—"reading, (w)riting and 'rithmetic." When they studied arithmetic, they might have learned measurements. Because the 13 colonies were British, traditional British measurements were used. Some of them sound pretty strange to us today: firkins, pottles, pinches, and sacks. Let's compare a colonial recipe with how it would look today. Also read aloud the F.U.N. Facts—Georgia, locate the colony on the *Jump Back* Map of Colonial America, and color it with pink and green stripes. For this station you will need:

- These instructions

- Copy of "Firkin, Pottle, Pinch, and Sack" for each student

- Pencil or pen

- Copy of F.U.N. Facts—Georgia for each child

- Pink and green pencils, crayons, or markers

TIPS FOR EXTRA FUN

- If your station timing allows, make Johnny Cakes. If not, discuss the recipe and do the calculations. Johnny Cakes also make a great end-of-day treat.

- Discuss the use of different measurements from other countries in colonial days—German, Irish, Scottish, French, Spanish, etc.—and how it might have complicated everyday life.

Firkin, Pottle, Pinch, and Sack

Have you ever been told to add a **pinch** of salt when you're cooking? In colonial days, a pinch was a real measurement. And you could also measure a pinch of water!

For very large amounts of dry things, colonists used measurements that sound strange to us. One **bushel** (32 quarts) measured grain and fruit. A **sack** measured flour and salt. But it was based on volume, not weight, so a sack of flour weighed 100 pounds while a sack of salt weighed 215 pounds.

Firkins (7.875 gallons) were used to measure some wet things like oil. Other liquids were measured in **hogsheads**, but varied by what was being measured. One hogshead of cider was 60 gallons, while a hogshead of honey was 63 gallons. A **pottle** was ½ gallon.

Some measurements could be used for either dry items or liquids. A **barrel** was 105 dry **quarts**, but don't forget to multiply a dry quart by 1.16 to equal a **wet quart**. Meanwhile, 2 **dashes** equals one **pinch** (⅟₈₄ of a fluid ounce or ⅟₁₆ of a dry teaspoon), which brings us back to cooking.

Here are some cooking measurements we use today. Let's try to figure out what a modern recipe would look like using colonial measurements.

1 teaspoon	= ⅓ of a tablespoon or ⅟₄₈ of a cup or ⅙ fluid ounce
1 tablespoon	= 3 teaspoons
1 cup	= 16 tablespoons or 8 fluid ounces
1 quart	= 4 cups or ¼ gallon or 32 fluid ounces
1 gallon	= 4 quarts

Johnny Cakes (makes 12 cakes)

Johnny Cakes were often called "journey cakes" because they could be taken on a journey or made along the way. To make Johnny Cakes, you will need:

2 cups oatmeal

How much of a bushel do you need? 1 bushel = 32 dry quarts

Math: 4 cups in 1 quart

$\times$ 32 quarts

128 cups in one bushel divided by the 2 cups _____ of a bushel

1 tsp salt

1 pinch = $\frac{1}{16}$ teaspoon _____ pinches

2 T oil

How many firkins do you need? 1 firkin = 3.875 gallons

Math: 16 tablespoons per cup

$\times$ 4 cups to the quart = 64 tablespoons in a quart

$\times$ 4 quarts to the gallon = 256 tablespoons in a gallon

$\times$ 3.875 gallons cups = 992 tablespoons in a firkin

divide by 2 tablespoons _____ of a firkin

1 cup water

How many pottles do you need? 1 pottle = $\frac{1}{2}$ gallon

Math: 1 quart $\times$ 4 = 4 cups in a quart $\times$ 2 for $\frac{1}{2}$ gallon

8 cups in a pottle; 1 cup = _____ of a pottle

$\frac{1}{2}$ cup milk

How many pottles do you need? 8 cups = 1 pottle

Divide by 2 for $\frac{1}{2}$ cup _____ of a pottle

1 cup maple syrup

How many hogsheads would you need if it was honey?

(63 gallons of honey to a hogshead)

Math: 4 cups in a quart

$\times$ 4 quarts in a gallon = 16 cups in a gallon

$\times$ 63 gallons = 1,008 cups in a hogshead

1 cup = _____ of a hogshead

Mixing bowl, spoon, griddle, pancake turner, and extra oil for griddle

Mix all ingredients except syrup in bowl until smooth. Oil griddle slightly. Spoon batter onto hot griddle. Fry on each side until golden brown. cool slightly. Serve alone or with maple syrup. Wouldn't 1,536 dashes of apple cider go nicely with those Johnny Cakes?

F.U.N. FACTS—Georgia

Famous People: In England, people who owed money (debtors) had to go to prison if they couldn't pay. King George II granted the land of Georgia to **General James Edward Oglethorpe** as a place for debtors to go instead of prison. General Oglethorpe brought soldiers to Georgia to protect the British colonies from Spanish settlements in Florida.

Unusual Tidbit: Indoor plumbing didn't exist in colonial times—no running water, no bathtubs, no toilets. Instead, people built special buildings outside near the house, called "outhouses" or "necessaries." Inside was a deep hole where people did their "necessary business." At night, nobody wanted to go outside in the cold, so they kept a pan underneath their bed or in the closet, called a "chamber pot," which they emptied in the morning.

Number: 4—Georgia was the fourth colony to become a state. Locate Georgia on your *Jump Back* Map of Colonial America and color it with pink and green stripes.

COLONIAL BUSINESS AND SCHOOL LIFE

Station 5. Fine Feathered Pens

The very first settlers who landed in Jamestown, Virginia, were businessmen, sent by British companies to find and ship back gold, minerals, fur, and lumber. After other settlers began to make the colonies their home, they brought their skills and set up businesses to provide goods and services to the colonists.

People didn't have computers or typewriters or even ballpoint pens to write with. Instead, they dipped the sharp tip of feathers (quills) into ink and scratched out their letters, lists, and documents. They folded the papers closed and placed a few drops of wax onto the edge of the papers to seal them shut. Then they pressed a brass stamp into the soft wax that left a design, like a cookie cutter. Before making quills, read aloud the F.U.N. Facts—Connecticut, locate the colony on the *Jump Back* Map of Colonial America, and color it green. At this station you will need:

- These instructions

- A stiff feather (turkey or pheasant feathers work well) for each child

- Sharp scissors

- Ink or thinned black paint

- Sheet of paper

- Paper towels

- Copy of F.U.N. Facts—Connecticut for each child

- Green pencils, crayons, or markers

Soak tips of feathers in water ahead of time to soften. Using scissors, cut the tip at a slant, then dip into ink or paint. The hollow part of the quill will hold the ink. The slanted point is used to write on the paper. If the point becomes dull, re-cut it just above the end. Practice writing your name, numbers, or the alphabet or imagine living in colonial days and write a letter to a friend.

TIPS FOR EXTRA FUN

- Fold the paper in thirds and use sealing wax to close. A type of store-bought sealing wax can be used in a low-temp glue gun but be careful as the gun tip may be hot. Press decorative buttons into the hot wax.

- Make your own sealing wax ahead of time or as a separate activity. Microwave ½ ounce of beeswax, 3 ounces of shellac flakes, and dry artist pigment to color until melted, stirring every 30 seconds. Pour into greased aluminum foil, roll to mold, and let cool. To use, hold a flame next to the wax and allow it to drip onto the paper. Wait a few seconds and press with a wet seal.

- Ask sportsman clubs for turkey or pheasant feathers or purchase them from a craft store.

- Lead a discussion of what seals meant: way to close envelopes without glue; gave important papers authority; sometimes signet rings were used (ring worn that had the wearer's initials or special design that was recognized by others).

F.U.N. FACTS—Connecticut

Famous People: Jonathan Trumbull was the British governor of Connecticut at the time the colonies declared their independence. He was the only colonial (British) governor who supported American independence from England.

Unusual Tidbit: A "buck" is a word we use to mean a dollar. In colonial America, a buckskin (the skin of a male deer) was worth about a dollar. The term "buck" was named for the deer that the money bought.

Number: 5—Connecticut was the fifth colony to become a state. Locate Connecticut on your *Jump Back* Map of Colonial America and color it green.

Station 6. Tinkering with Tin

In colonial times, to make candlelight special, people would sometimes place the candles inside or behind special covers. Holes were punched in the metal covers so that candlelight shone through the holes in designs. While making the tin art, read aloud the F.U.N. Facts—Massachusetts, locate the colony on the *Jump Back* Map of Colonial America, and color it blue. At this station you will need:

- These instructions
- Foil casserole pans (1" × 6" × 8" cut in half lengthwise—one pan makes 2 projects)
- Cardboard or wood
- Hammers or mallets
- Nails
- 2 brass brads for each candle cover
- Paper, pencil, tape, scissors
- Copy of F.U.N. Facts—Massachusetts for each child
- Blue pencils, crayons, or markers

Precut foil pans in half lengthwise. Have children cut edges from the 2 short sides, leaving the rim along one side for the bottom of the candle cover. Have children sketch a pattern on the sheet of paper and tape it to the foil. Place the foil on heavy cardboard or wood to protect the table. Punch holes through both the paper and the tin with the hammer and nail—leaving spaces between the holes but following the lines of the pattern as if creating a connect-the-dot puzzle. Remove the tape and paper. Punch 2 additional holes at the top and 2 at the bottom corners. Roll the foil gently and fasten with 2 brass brads, snipping rim if needed to allow it to curve. When the cover is placed over a lit candle, the pattern will shine through.

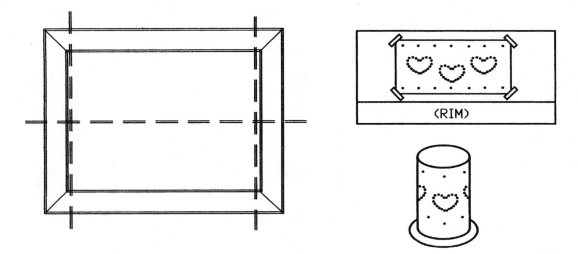

Punched Tin Art

TIPS FOR EXTRA FUN

- Popular colonial designs were hearts, pineapples, crosses, and animals.
- As an alternative, foil pie plates can be punched and hung as decorations.

F.U.N. FACTS—Massachusetts

Famous People: **Pilgrims** were the first European people to settle America permanently. They arrived at Plymouth, Massachusetts, on the ship, *Mayflower*. Although they were originally from England, the Pilgrims had spent years living in Holland because English law didn't allow them to practice their religion. They came to America to worship freely.

Unusual Tidbit: People wore little bouquets of flowers on their collar or shoulders near their noses to keep from smelling other peoples' body odor! The little bouquets were called "nosegays" because they made their noses happy!

Number: 6—Massachusetts was the sixth colony to become a state. Locate Massachusetts on your *Jump Back* Map of Colonial America and color it blue.

Station 7. Honk, Honk? No, Moo!

Colonial school was one room for everybody—one teacher taught all the children regardless of their ages or how much education they had. There were no white boards and paper was very expensive. Some students wrote on slate (a dark stone) or wrote with coal on wood, but most students practiced their writing on "hornbooks." Hornbooks were a wooden paddle. A piece of animal horn, often from a cow, boiled and scraped thin enough to see through covered a sheet of paper on the paddle. The paper had the letters of the alphabet and a saying or Bible verse written on it. The children practiced writing on the clear animal horn covering, wiped it clean, and used it again. The horn covering gave the paddle the name of "hornbook." While making hornbooks, read aloud the F.U.N. Facts—Maryland, locate the colony on the *Jump Back* Map of Colonial America, and color it pink. At this station you will need:

- These instructions
- 8" × 11" poster board or cardboard
- ½ sheet of plain paper (precut)
- Plastic wrap
- Scissors
- Dry erase markers
- Tape
- Paper towels
- Copy of F.U.N. Facts—Maryland for each child
- Pink pencils, crayons, or markers

Following the general shape indicated, have children cut out a cardboard hornbook. Have children write upper and lower case letters on the ½ sheet of paper and tape it to the cardboard. Cut a length of plastic long enough to cover the front of the hornbook and wrap around the sides and top. Tape the plastic to the back of the hornbook, leaving the handle uncovered. Using dry-erase markers, children can practice tracing letters and wiping them clean with the paper towels.

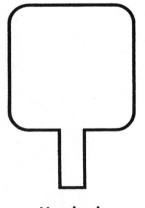

Hornbook

TIPS FOR EXTRA FUN

- Use colored paper and cardboard.
- Think up unusual or funny sayings to copy. Colonial kids often used Bible verses.

F.U.N. FACTS—Maryland

Famous People: It was against the law in England to practice the Roman Catholic religion. King Charles I granted the colony of Maryland to **Sir George Calvert** for Roman Catholics to settle. Two ships, the *Ark* and the *Dove* brought the first Catholic settlers to Maryland. Maryland passed the first colonial law granting religious freedom.

Unusual Tidbit: Before wealthy colonists arrived in America with fine dishes, colonists carved bowls (trenches) right into the top of rough wooden tables. Food was placed inside the bowl and after dinner, the whole thing could be wiped out. No dishes to wash; nothing to put away. Easy, right? Yes, but the wood was hard to clean and bacteria and bugs caused diseases, including one called "trench mouth." Still, colonial kids never complained about loading the dishwasher!

Number: 7—Maryland was the seventh colony to become a state. Locate Maryland on your *Jump Back* Map of Colonial America and color it pink.

COLONIAL LIVING

Station 8. What Time Is It? Check Your Sundial

Since ancient times, sundials have been one way people could keep track of time. Sundials don't need electricity. They don't need batteries. They simply have to sit in the sunshine. By noting where the sun's shadow fell on the sundial, colonial people had a good idea of what time it was. For a sundial to really be accurate, it and the triangular pointer, called a gnomon (NO-mehn), must be adjusted to your specific location and time of year. Our sundials (meant for the Northern Hemisphere) will therefore not be accurate, but we can understand how sundials work and can watch the sun's path by observing the shadows. While making the sundials, read aloud the F.U.N. Facts—South Carolina, locate the colony on the *Jump Back* Map of Colonial America, and color it with blue and green stripes. At this station you will need:

- These instructions

- 1 heavy 10½" paper plate for each sundial

- 45-degree triangle of poster board (4" at base)

- Duct or other heavy tape

- Pencil

- Ruler

- Watch

- Copy of F.U.N. Facts—South Carolina for each child

- Blue and green pencils, crayons, or markers

This project should be done outdoors. Using a ruler and pencil or marker, divide the circle into 4 quarters. Write a "12" at the top and bottom end of one line. Write a "6" at the left and right end of the second line. Find the midpoint between the left hand "6" and the bottom "12" and write a number "3." Find the mid point between the right hand "6" and the bottom "12" and write a number "9." Fill in

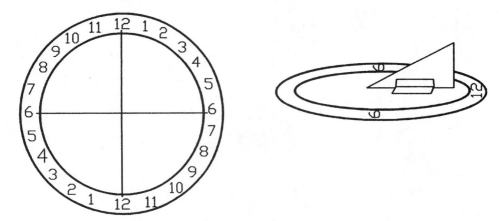

Sundial

remaining numbers. Cut a right triangle with a 4" base from poster board and tape it in the center of the plate so that it stands up vertically above the plate, with the tip pointing away from the bottom "12". Note the time. Turn the sundial so the triangle forms a shadow on the number closest to the current time.

TIPS FOR EXTRA FUN

- Decorate the sundials.

- If it is not sunny outside, use a lamp or very bright flashlight. Although this will not be helpful in telling time, it will illustrate the connection between the sun's position and shadows. Shine the lamp from directly overhead and from different directions to simulate the sun at different times of day. Check the shadow.

- Have everyone leave their sundials outside (make sure names are on them). Recheck sundials and note shadows throughout the day (recess, lunch, end of day). If it is windy, place a rock on the plate to weigh it down.

- Lead a discussion—how latitude, seasons, and weather affect sundials. Most sundials have no numbers to show the time between 8 P.M. and 4 A.M. Why not? The sun is not out at night!

F.U.N. FACTS—South Carolina

Famous People: Elizabeth "Eliza" Lucas was the first important agriculturalist in the United States. She moved from the Caribbean to South Carolina when she was young. As a teenager she began to run her father's plantation and saw that the textile (fabric) industry would provide wealth for the southern colonies. She knew about indigo (a plant that makes a blue dye for fabric) that grew in the Caribbean. She experimented with growing indigo in South Carolina until she produced a type of plant that could grow there. Indigo became an important source of money for South Carolina and other southern colonies. George Washington was one of the people who helped carry Eliza Lucas' coffin when she died.

Unusual Tidbit: Stockades were used to punish people for crimes. Wooden boards were made with spaces for a head, hands, and sometimes feet. The person's head and hands were locked inside so he couldn't escape. The stockades were placed outside in a public place. The biggest part of the punishment was embarrassment. People would laugh or shout at the prisoner—and often throw rotten food at him!

Number: 8—South Carolina was the eighth colony to become a state. Locate South Carolina on your *Jump Back* Map of Colonial America and color it with blue and green stripes.

Station 9. The Rooster Says a Storm Is Coming

People who forecast weather describe the wind direction as where it is coming FROM. Generally, in America cold winter storms come from the north. During planting times it is important for farmers to understand weather, including wind direction, which sometimes helps tell what kind of weather is coming.

Many colonists had weathervanes on top of their houses or barns. The base of the weathervane has four compass points pointing toward north, south, east, and west. One half of the weathervane is heavier than the other half. As the wind blows against the weathervane, the light end turns into the wind and the heavy end turns away from the wind. So just by looking at the weathervane, colonists could tell the direction of the wind. Often, these colonial weathervanes were very decorative. While making weathervanes, read aloud the F.U.N. Facts—New Hampshire, locate the colony on the *Jump Back* Map of Colonial America, and color it with red and yellow stripes. At this station you will need:

- These instructions
- 8½" × 11" construction paper
- Plastic drinking straws
- Straightened coat hangers or other stiff wire (about 14–16")
- Wire cutters
- Soda bottles (20 oz.) with plastic screw tops
- Heavy nails
- Hammers
- Wood blocks
- Sand or small pebbles
- Scissors
- Glue
- Pencils
- Small washers or paperclips
- Duct or masking tape
- Strips of paper approximately 3–4" wide
- Black markers
- Compass
- Copy of F.U.N. Facts—New Hampshire for each child
- Red and yellow pencils, crayons, or markers

Fold a sheet of 8½" × 11" construction paper in half to make a 8½" × 5½" rectangle. Sketch a simple figure on one side and cut to make two identical shapes. Find the approximate center of the shape and tape the drinking straw to the inside of one shape so the straw extends below the shape by 1–2". Snip off any extra straw that extends beyond the top. Tape over the top end of the drinking straw to block it. Tape the washer or paperclip to the inside back end of the shape and glue the second shape to the first, matching edges.

Partly fill the soda bottle with sand or pebbles to make a sturdy base. Cut and tape a band of paper around the bottle and tape it securely. With a marker, write a large N on the paper on one side of the bottle; an E, an S, and a W equidistant around the bottle to form a compass.

Hammer a nail through the center of the bottle cap on the wooden block. Remove the nail and replace the cap. Cut a length of wire the height of the bottle plus the height of the shape. Insert the wire through the bottle cap and into the sand or pebbles. Slide the shape over the wire using the straw as a sleeve so the shape spins freely.

Place your weathervane outside pointing your bottle north. If you don't have a compass, think about which direction the sun rises (east) and sets (west). To aim your weathervane north, east will be on your right and west will be on your left. The back part of your figure is heavier because the washer or paperclip causes wind resistance. Therefore your weathervane should point the direction the wind comes FROM.

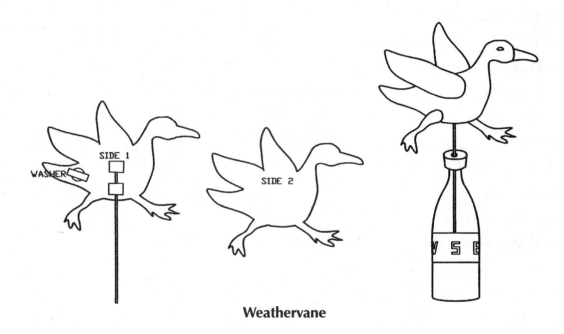

Weathervane

TIPS FOR EXTRA FUN

- If there is a strong wind outside, try tossing a few blades of grass into the air to check the wind direction or lick your finger and stick it into the air and feel the wind.

- Use bright colors and leave enough space so the shape can spin easily over the bottle.

- Set your weathervane outside your classroom or in your yard and check the wind direction daily. Keep a record.

- If you have too much weight at the front of your weathervane, it may just spin or turn sideways. Try repositioning the weight until it points correctly.

F.U.N. FACTS—New Hampshire

Famous People: The colony of New Hampshire was nothing but several fishing settlements until **Reverend John Wheelwright** and his religious followers settled the town of Exeter. New Hampshire remained unsettled for a long time because many different people claimed they owned the same land.

Unusual Tidbit: Cameras hadn't been invented in colonial times so people had portraits painted by artists. To make things quicker, artists called "limners" traveled from town to town carrying canvases with partially completed pictures. If someone wanted a portrait, the limner only had to fill in the face. This explains why you might see several portraits of different people all wearing the same clothes. It was Colonial America's answer to digital cameras!

Number: 9—New Hampshire was the ninth colony to become a state. Locate New Hampshire on your *Jump Back* Map of Colonial America and color it with red and yellow stripes.

Station 10. Curly Qs

"Quilling" was a type of decorative art popular in colonial times. People made designs by curling strips of paper around quill pens. These lacy designs also hung as mobiles or on Christmas trees. Before quilling, read aloud the F.U.N. Facts—Virginia, locate the colony on the *Jump Back* Map of Colonial America, and color it with purple and orange stripes. At this station you will need:

- These instructions

- White or colored paper (heavy paper does not curl well)

- Scissors

- Pencil

- String

- Glue

- Copy of F.U.N. Facts—Virginia for each child

- Purple and orange pencils, crayons, or markers

Cut several strips of paper approximately ¼" wide and several inches long. Wrap around a pencil to curl. Make shapes by gluing one end to a piece of paper or hang a shape from a string as decoration. To form a heart, make a "V" shape out of one length of paper by pinching it at the center and then curling the 2 ends inward. Form birds and butterflies or bugs with wings and antennas.

Quilling Designs

TIPS FOR EXTRA FUN

- Make a card for a teacher, friend, or family member for an upcoming holiday (Valentine's Day, Mother's Day, Father's Day, Halloween, Thanksgiving, Christmas, or other holiday).

- Make a mobile—you will need sticks for crossbars and extra string.

- Make hanging decorations.

F.U.N. FACTS—Virginia

Famous People: King James of England granted the London Company the right to settle Virginia. In 1607, the London Company sent the first people to form a settlement at Jamestown to find and ship back gold, trees for lumber, and other valuable products. **Captain John Smith** was one of the early leaders at Jamestown and helped the settlers and the Powhatan Indians become friends.

Unusual Tidbit: There was no central heating in colonial times. Hot air rises so it is colder near the floor. In colonial times beds were built high (where it was warmer) and people often had to climb up a few steps to get into bed. Even today we "climb into bed."

Number: 10—Virginia was the tenth colony to become a state. Locate Virginia on your *Jump Back* Map of Colonial America and color it with purple and orange stripes.

COLONIAL FUN AND GAMES

Station 11. Jolly Jumpers

When "jumping jack puppets" came to colonial America from France, they became one of the most popular colonial toys. While making jolly jumpers, read aloud the F.U.N. Facts—New York, locate the colony on the *Jump Back* Map of Colonial America, and color it with red and blue stripes. At this station you will need:

- These instructions
- Copies of *Jump Back* Jolly Jumper pattern
- Card stock
- String
- 8 brass paper fasteners for each jumper
- Pencil, ruler, scissors, sharp nail, glue, tape
- Scraps of fabric, lace, buttons, beads, crayons, markers
- Copy of F.U.N. Facts—New York for each child
- Red and blue pencils, crayons, or markers

Trace the body, legs, and arms on card stock and cut out. Using the nail, carefully punch holes where the dots are shown on the pattern. Decorate the figure pieces.

Tape ends of string and thread a 6" piece of string through the hole at the top of the head and tie.

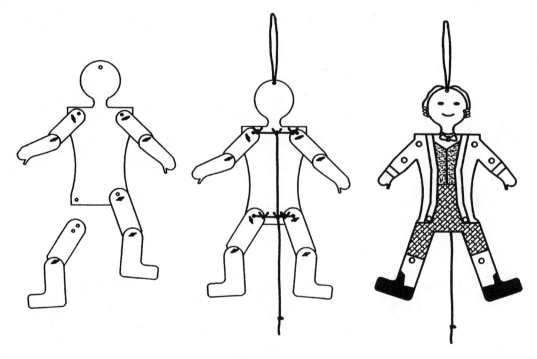

Jolly Jumper

Attach the arm sections at elbows and the leg sections at knees with fasteners (prongs to the back). Attach arms and legs with fasteners to the body at the second hole from the top.

Place jumper face down. Connect the 2 upper holes on the arms with an 8" string. Connect the 2 upper holes on the legs with an 8" string. Snip off any extra string. Tie a 12" string vertically to both the horizontal arm string and the horizontal leg string, letting it hang about 3" past the feet. Holding the head string in one hand, pull down on the bottom string to make him dance.

TIPS FOR EXTRA FUN

- Decorate the jumpers in colonial attire or as a famous colonial or revolutionary figure (George Washington, Benjamin Franklin, Betsy Ross).

- Put on a puppet show.

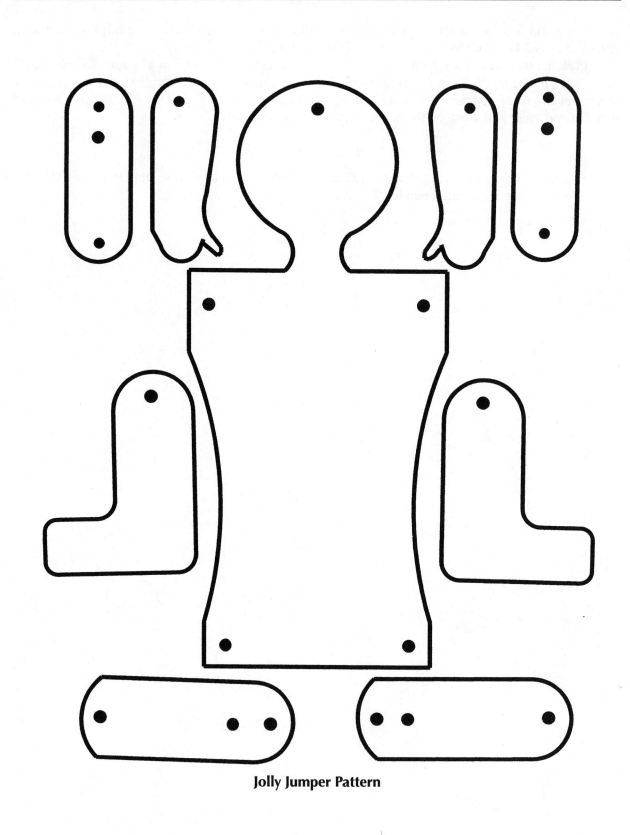

Jolly Jumper Pattern

F.U.N. FACTS—New York

Famous People: New York was first settled by the Dutch, who named the area "New Netherlands" (Netherlands is the name of the country where the Dutch people live). They named New York City "New Amsterdam." While England was fighting the Dutch in Europe the English **Duke of York** sent a fleet of ships to New Netherlands. The Dutch governor **Peter Stuyvesant** surrendered without a fight. The colony and the city were renamed New York after the Duke of York (King Charles II's brother).

Unusual Tidbit: In colonial times, mattresses were placed over ropes attached to the bed frame. When the ropes started to sag, they had to be tightened with a wrench. That's why we say "sleep tight" when we go to bed.

Number: 11—New York was the eleventh colony to become a state. Locate New York on your *Jump Back* Map of Colonial America and color it with red and blue stripes.

Station 12. Nine Men's Morris

The game of Nine Men's Morris was a popular board game in colonial America. Before playing the game, read aloud the F.U.N. Facts—North Carolina, locate the colony on the *Jump Back* Map of Colonial America, and color it with yellow and blue stripes. At this station you will need:

- These instructions

- Copies of Nine Men's Morris game board (1 for every 2 players)

- 9 game pieces per child (dried beans, paperclips, etc., but the 2 sets of pieces per game should be different to identify the players)

- Copy of F.U.N. Facts—North Carolina for each child

- Yellow and blue pencils, crayons, or markers

To play the game, the person with the first name alphabetically starts. Each player takes turns placing the game pieces one at a time on the game board circles. The object is to get 3 pieces in a row while preventing the other person from doing so. When you get 3 in a row, you take one of your opponent's game pieces off the board. The one with game pieces remaining is the winner.

TIPS FOR EXTRA FUN

- If there is time to play several games, try different strategies—starting from different points on the board, for example.

- Winners of each game can have a play-off until there is an ultimate winner for the group.

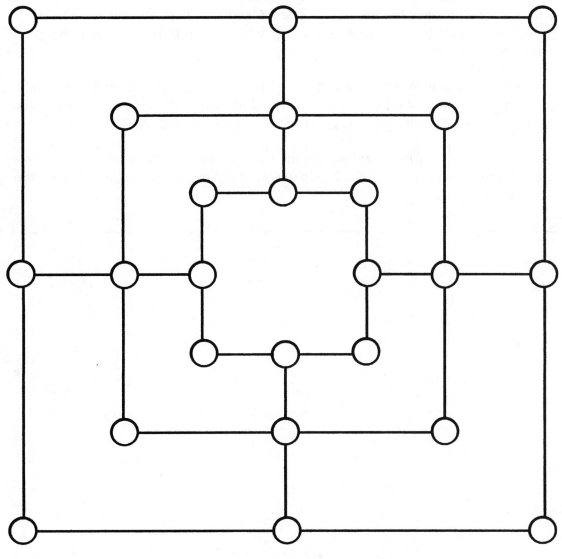

Nine Men's Morris Game Board

F.U.N. FACTS—North Carolina

Famous People: King Charles II of England granted the land of North Carolina to eight English gentlemen who helped him regain his throne. Seven of the gentlemen sold off their property but the eighth, **Lord Granville**, kept his interest. The name "Carolina" comes from the word "Carolus," which is Latin for Charles, in honor of King Charles I.

Unusual Tidbit: Women couldn't go to the department store for makeup in colonial days. Instead they used chimney soot to darken their lashes and eyebrows and crushed a type of beetle (yes—a bug!) to redden their lips and cheeks.

Number: 12—North Carolina was the twelfth colony to become a state. Locate North Carolina on your *Jump Back* Map of Colonial America and color it with yellow and blue stripes.

Station 13. Top It Off!

Tops were popular toys in colonial America. Most children made their own tops. While making tops, read aloud the F.U.N. Facts—Rhode Island, locate the colony on the *Jump Back* Map of Colonial America, and color it orange. At this station you will need:

- These instructions

- Poster board or card stock

- Pencils

- Circle pattern (jar top or other circle approximately 3" in diameter)

- Scissors

- Nails for poking—should be slightly narrower than a toothpick

- Round toothpicks

- Copy of F.U.N. Facts—Rhode Island for each child

- Orange pencils, crayons, or markers

Trace a circle on the poster board or card stock and cut out. Poke the nail into the center of the circle and insert the toothpick so that the circle sits at approximately the center of the toothpick. Hold the top of the toothpick between your thumb and forefinger, spin, and let go. Adjust the circle closer to or farther away from the tip as needed.

TIPS FOR EXTRA FUN

- Use marker pens to color or make designs on the circles and watch them spin.

- Draw a large circle on the ground and divide it into 10 sections. Number them randomly, but number 1 should be the largest section and number 10 should be the smallest. One by one, set spinning tops in the middle of the circle. Score by the number the top lands on.

- See who can keep their top spinning longest.

F.U.N. FACTS—Rhode Island

Famous People: Roger Williams was a minister who had been kicked out of Massachusetts by the Puritans because he had different religious beliefs. He bought the land that is now the city of Providence, Rhode Island, from the Indians and soon the colony became a place where other settlers went for religious freedom. **Anne Hutchinson** was one of the later settlers who came to Rhode Island. She believed women had a right to speak at worship services.

Unusual Tidbit: Colonists cooked in huge fireplaces. There might be several pots of food cooking over the fire and a spit (a long metal pole) with a roast or whole turkey on it. Next to the fireplace might be a wheel connected to the pole with a cage around it. A small dog inside the cage ran around like a hamster on a wheel. As he ran, the wheel turned the spit, and rotated the meat to cook it evenly. These dogs were called "turnspit dogs."

Number: 13—Rhode Island was the thirteenth colony to become a state. Locate Rhode Island on your *Jump Back* Map and color it orange.

END THE DAY AS A GROUP

Station 14. Quick Quoits

One of the most popular games in colonial times was quoits (KWAITS). This game is similar to our game of horseshoes and was originally brought to America by English settlers. In quoits, heavy metal or rope rings were tossed instead of horseshoes. This game should be played outside on a large lawn. For each game of quoits you will need:

- These instructions
- Two sturdy wooden pegs approximately 10" long
- 4 rings made ahead of time. Either tie stiff rope (approximately 12" long) into a ring or cut rings from a thoroughly washed-out plastic bleach bottle (soda bottles are too lightweight). If cutting rings from bleach bottles, use a handsaw or heavy serrated kitchen knife.
- Rubber mallet or hammer
- Paper and pencil for scoring

Hammer the pegs (called "hobs") into the grass approximately 5' from each other. Make a mark about 4' from the hob. Players line up behind one hob and toss rings, one at a time, at the other hob. Score one point for each ring that lands on the hob. All players take turns and the winners have a playoff.

TIPS FOR EXTRA FUN

- Set up 2 or more quoit fields and have team challenges.
- Set out 3 or 4 additional hobs at different distances. Score the closer hob 1, the next hob 2, and so forth, giving the highest score to the hob farthest away.
- You can make 4–6 rings from one large bleach bottle; plan to have a few extras on hand.

Station 15. Nine Pin

Colonists originally brought the game of nine pin (also called "skittles") over with them from Germany and the Netherlands. It was played outside on a long board or flat ground by rolling a wooden ball to knock down a set of wooden pins. You score one point for each pin that is knocked down. After ten turns, the person with the most points wins.

Does nine pin sound like bowling? In some places, nine pin was so popular that people became rowdy and some of the colonies outlawed the game. So people added another pin to the game, changed the name to "ten pin," and kept playing! Ten pin became our game of bowling. To play nine pin you will need:

- These instructions
- Nine empty soda bottles (partially filled with sand if it is windy)
- Rubber ball
- Masking tape (if playing inside) or chalk (if playing outside)
- Paper and pencil for scoring

Play this outside on flat ground or indoors in a large open room. Mark a diamond-shaped formation on the ground with chalk or on the floor with tape according to the diagram. Set the bottles on the marks. Mark off a starting line approximately 10' from the first pin. Players line up behind that line and take turns rolling the ball toward the pin. After taking a turn, the player is responsible for resetting the pins for the next player. Players take turns rolling and counting the number of pins they knock down—one roll of the ball per turn. The player with the highest score after ten rolls wins.

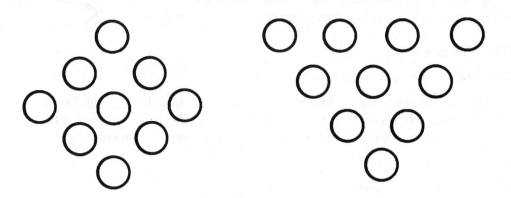

NINE PIN BOWLING
FORMATION

TEN PIN BOWLING
FORMATION

Nine and Ten Pin Formations

TIPS FOR EXTRA FUN

- This game can be played alternating with quoits. After the player has taken a turn at nine pin, a turn can then be taken at quoits; or players can rotate in groups.

- If time is short, limit the number of turns per person.

- Set up more nine pin games for less waiting.

Station 16. Thanksgiving Fun

Assemble souvenir booklets and take photographs in front of the quilt murals at this station (see Chapter 1 tips for booklets and group photographs). Provide some of the following foods for snacks:

Roasted turkey slices rolled up with toothpicks

Fresh berries or fruit

Nuts

Pumpkin bread (see recipe)

Pumpkin soup (see recipe)

Apple cider

Cornmeal mush with maple syrup

Dried apple slices

Candied orange peel

Dried fruit mashed into paste and dried—like our fruit rollups

Smoked meat and fish

Hominy—dried corn soaked in mixture of water and ashes; rinsed and stir fried

Pemmican

Hardtack

Rock candy—make it as an activity for schools

Powhanton apone (corn cakes)—mix 2 cups corn meal; ½ cup bear fat (or shortening!); ½ cup of dried fruit, fresh corn, or nuts. Add boiling water until moist (¼–½ cup); fry on hot slate over a campfire (or use a griddle!)

Cups, spoons, plates, napkins

TIPS FOR EXTRA FUN

- Switch this station to midday for a lunchtime feast.
- Lead a discussion about the first Thanksgiving.
- Lead a discussion about how colonists had to learn about new foods.
- SMILE!

Recipes

Jump Back Pumpkin Soup

(4 Servings or 8–12 samples)

Pumpkins stayed fresh longer in winter when other vegetables were not available and could be dried to use later. Stir and heat (do not boil) the following in a saucepan. Serve hot.

One 16-ounce can pumpkin

3 cups milk

1 teaspoon salt

1 teaspoon cinnamon

1 teaspoon ground nutmeg

¼ teaspoon ground clove

JUMP BACK PUMPKIN BREAD

(4 large loaves—48 slices)

In a large bowl, combine:

3⅓ cup flour

2 teaspoons baking soda

1½ teaspoon salt

1 teaspoon cinnamon

1 teaspoon nutmeg

3 cups sugar

Make a hole in the above dry ingredients, add the following, and mix until smooth:

1 cup oil

4 eggs

⅔ cup water

2 cups canned pumpkin

Pour into four ungreased loaf pans and bake for 1 hour at 350 degrees. Cool before slicing.

Chapter 5

Pioneer Day

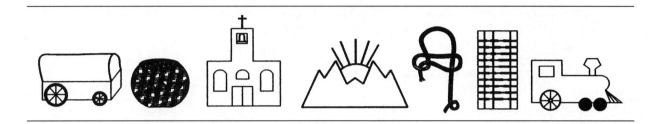

Welcome to Pioneer Day. During this day of fun, children will rotate through stations learning about U.S. westward expansion. They will start the day as a single group, participating in organizational activities to gear them up for learning. Then they will split into smaller groups, rotate through stations, and join up again at the end of the day with activities to summarize what they've learned. The Pioneer Day stations and activities are:

Start the Day as a Group

Station 1. Music Hall (Pioneer Songs, Gathering Bags, Grouping, and Nametags)

Westward Ho!—The Journey

Station 2. Blacksmith Shop (Learn about Wagons)

Station 3. On the Trail (Board Game)

Home on the Range—Life in the Old West

Station 4. Western Lasso and Rodeo Supply (Knot Tying)

Station 5. Better Butter Shop (Homemade Butter)

Mission Makers—Spanish Unit

Station 6. Old Adobe Cantina (Tortillas)

Station 7. Senior Zapata's Toy Shop (Piñatas)

Golden Legacy—Chinese Unit

Station 8. Wong's Diner (Chopstick Relay Race)

Station 9. Beaded Calculators (Abacus)

Hunters and Gatherers—Native American Unit

Station 10. Chumash Bank (Shell Money)

Station 11. Miwok Village (Shinny)

A New Way to Go—Railroads

Station 12. Railroad Station (Board Game)

Station 13. Telegraph Company (Morse Code)

End the Day as a Group

Station 14. Photography Palace and Print Shop (Group Photos and Souvenir Booklets)

NAMETAGS

Choose from the following or think of your own:

Padres	Dream Catchers	Miners
Seniors and Senoritas	Manchurians	Tumbleweeds
Gauchos	Dynasty Builders	Prairie Schooners
Buffalo Hunters	Railroad Builders	Pioneers
Braves	49-ers	Pony Express Riders
Bareback Riders	Golden Spikes	Stage Coach Drivers
Chiefs	Wagon Masters	Iron Horses
Basket Weavers	Mountaineers	Explorers
Straight Arrows	Trail Blazers	Buckaroos

COSTUME IDEAS

Costumes can be elaborate or as simple as a straw hat or a red bandana, aprons for girls, felt vests for boys (cut from one piece; little sewing required). Don't forget to incorporate other cultures relevant to the west. Props for photos might include ropes, shovels, or a big rock—spray painted gold!

START THE DAY AS A GROUP

Station 1. Music Hall

This station starts the day with everyone assembled. Instructions are given at this station and children are placed into groups and given their nametags. This station can also be combined with a visit from a historian or with reading legends and stories about pioneer life. Then sing songs about the Old West. Lyrics can be shown on an overhead or copies given as handouts. Children will also make a gathering bag for their handouts and projects they make throughout the day (see Chapter 1). At this station you will need:

- These instructions

- Music lyrics—either on overhead or copied for handouts

- Optional sing-along music (cassette or CD player) and access to electricity or a guitar/piano-playing leader

- Items for gathering bag (see Chapter 1)

TIPS FOR EXTRA FUN

- Homemade instruments (boxes, sticks, pan tops, spoons) work great!

- Play Old West music in the background on cassette or CD after the sing-a-long.

- Suggest kids decorate their gathering bags with a theme from one of the stations: the journey, life in the West, the railroad, or one of the cultures (Spanish, Chinese, Native American).

Buffalo Gals

Buffalo gals, won't you come out tonight,
Come out tonight, come out tonight?
Buffalo gals, won't you come out tonight,
And dance by the light of the moon?

I danced with a gal with a hole in her stockin',
And her heel kep' a-rockin' and her toe kep' a-knockin',
I danced with a gal with a hole in her stockin',
And we danced by the light of the moon.

I asked her if she'd stop and talk,
Stop and talk, stop and talk.
Her feet covered up the whole sidewalk,
she was fair to view.

I asked her if she'd stop and dance,
Have a dance, care to dance,
I thought that I might get a chance
to shake a foot with her.

I asked her if she'd be my wife,
be my wife, be my wife.
Then I'd be happy all my life
if she would marry me.

I danced with the dolly with a hole in her stocking,
And her feet kept a-rocking and her knees kept a-knocking.
O I danced with the dolly with a hole in her stocking
And we danced by the light of the moon.

I've Been Workin' on the Railroad

I've been workin' on the railroad,
All the live long day.
I've been workin' on the railroad,
Just to pass the time away.
Don't you hear the whistle blowing?
Rise up so early in the morn.
Don't you hear the captain shouting
"Dinah, blow your horn?"

   Dinah, won't you blow,
   Dinah, won't you blow,
   Dinah, won't you blow your horn?
   Dinah, won't you blow,
   Dinah, won't you blow,
   Dinah, won't you blow your horn?

Someone's in the kitchen with Dinah.
Someone's in the kitchen, I know.
Someone's in the kitchen with Dinah
Strumming on the old banjo.
Fee, fie, fiddle-e-I-o.
Fee, fie, fiddle-e-I-o-o-o-o.
Fee, fie, fiddle-e-I-o.
Strumming on the old banjo.

Clementine

In a cavern, in a canyon,
Excavating for a mine,
Dwelt a miner, forty-niner,
And his daughter Clementine.

CHORUS
Oh my darling, oh my darling,
Oh my darling, Clementine,
Thou art lost and gone forever,
Dreadful sorry, Clementine.

Light she was and like a fairy,
And her shoes were number nine,
Herring boxes without topses,
Sandals were for Clementine.

CHORUS
Drove she ducklings to the water
Every morning just at nine,
Hit her foot against a splinter,
Fell into the foaming brine.

CHORUS
Ruby lips above the water,
Blowing bubbles soft and fine,
But alas, I was no swimmer,
So I lost my Clementine.

CHORUS
Then the miner, forty-niner
Soon began to peak and pine,
Thought he oughter jine he daughter,
Now he's with his Clementine.

CHORUS
In my dreams she still doth haunt me,
Robed in garments soaked in brine,
Though in life I used to hug her,
Now she's dead, I draw the line.

WESTWARD HO!—THE JOURNEY

Station 2. Blacksmith Shop

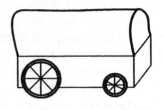

One of the first stops for pioneers heading west was the wagon builder and blacksmith shop. This station introduces kids to pioneer wagons. Have children take turns reading "Hauling up Mountains, Tumbling down Mountains, and Riding Rivers" and the handout "Wacky Wagon Why's." Combine discussions with making a communal mural for end-of-day photos. Use butcher paper or smaller sheets that can be taped together. Each group creates a scene from early pioneer life. Encourage kids to draw large and without too much detail. At this station you will need:

- These instructions

- "Hauling up Hills, Tumbling down Mountains, and Riding Rivers"

- Copy of "Wacky Wagon Why's" for each child as handout

- Butcher paper (approximately 10–12' long) or 1 sheet of poster board for each group

- Marker pens, crayons

TIPS FOR EXTRA FUN

- If using one poster board, write the group name at the top of the board.

- Floors make the best workspace.

- Encourage groups to decide on a scene before they start drawing—or have an adult assign each group a scene. Ideas: building the railroad, a portion of the journey west, a wagon, supplies, something about one of the cultures important in the settlement of the West, herd of buffalo, mountain scene, desert scene, prairie scene, crossing a river, a pioneer family.

Hauling Up Hills, Tumbling Down Mountains, and Riding Rivers

Two or three yokes of animals usually pulled wagons. One yoke is a set of two animals side by side. More than two yokes made the wagon and the team too long to turn through the hills and trees. Sometimes animals going uphill needed a rest. But if they stopped, the heavy wagon would pull them back down. So pioneers led animals part way up and tied the wagon to trees so the animals could rest a few moments before continuing up the mountain.

If the uphill trail was straight, families could share animals. Sometimes a dozen yoke of oxen (24 animals) were hitched to one wagon. When they reached the top, the animals were unhitched, brought back down the hill, and hitched to the next wagon. This was repeated until all the wagons were at the top. But sometimes the animals just couldn't make it. When there were large boulders blocking the trail, for example, the animals were unhitched and taken to the top. Then the men tied ropes to the wagon and lifted it up the hill.

Wagons didn't have good brakes. When wagons went downhill, sometimes the wheels had to be "locked" by tying a chain or rope through them to keep them from turning. Sometimes a cut tree was dragged behind the wagon like an anchor to slow it down. Sometimes, the wagon was unhitched from the team and lowered over a cliff with ropes.

Wagons were so heavy, there was danger that a wagon going downhill would slip free and run over the animals pulling it. So usually all but one yoke of oxen were unhooked from the wagon when it went downhill. Pioneers also made sure that only one wagon went down the mountain at a time to prevent a wagon from crashing into the wagons in front.

Pioneers had to cross many streams on their journey west. There was only about 2½ feet between the ground and the bottom of the wagon. Sometimes pioneers raised the wagon bed by putting blocks of wood between it and the axles to give them another foot of clearance. If a river was too deep, the wheels were removed and the wagon was floated across.

Some rivers had swift currents and sandy bottoms. Often animals were swept away by the current or wheels got stuck in the soft river bottoms. A ferry was built on the Platte River where crossing was dangerous. There, pioneers loaded the wagon and animals onto a raft attached to ropes. The raft was then pulled across the river by animals already on the other side.

Wacky Wagon Why's

The prairie schooner was the covered wagon used by most pioneers. It was about the size of a mini-van and could carry one and a half tons of supplies. It was a light wagon, which meant it got stuck less often in muddy streams and was easier for animals to pull. Another wagon, the Conestoga, could carry five tons of supplies. But it was made for traveling on the East Coast and was too heavy for travel where there were no roads.

There was little room inside wagons to sit or sleep, so most people walked the whole 2,000 miles. They ate outside and slept in tents or out under the stars. A cloth top covered tall wooden rails on the wagons and protected the contents from rain. The cloth might have been sealed with paint or oil to make it waterproof.

Most pioneers brought along an extra axle. The axle connected the wagon wheels to the yokes. If an axle broke and couldn't be replaced, pioneers had to leave their wagon and everything they owned and take only what they could carry or pack on their animals.

Rear wagon wheels were 5–6 feet in diameter to help the wagon roll over bumps and holes without getting stuck. The front wheels were smaller so they could turn without hitting the side of the wagon. The wide rims helped keep the wheels from sinking into mud.

Oxen worked in pairs called "yokes." The largest oxen were placed next to the wagon, where it was heaviest and hardest to pull. Many pioneers chose oxen for their strength, because they cost less, and because they could eat grass along the trail. Oxen could also be eaten in an emergency. Other pioneers chose mules or horses to pull wagons because they were faster than oxen. But mules and horses were expensive and pioneers also had to buy and carry food for them, which meant less room for their own supplies. Which would you choose?

Station 3. On the Trail

At this station children play a board game to learn about difficulties on the trail. The board game can be played by two or more. Show children the California/Oregon Trail location using the *Jump Back* Trail Map as a guide. Then divide children into groups. Each group should have one board game, one die, and one game piece for each player. At this station you will need:

- These instructions

- A large U.S. map (optional)

- One copy of *Jump Back* Trail Map to use as a guide

- Copy of On the Trail board game, enlarged as needed, for each child

- One die for each group of players

- Game pieces (buttons, slips of colored paper, dried beans, paperclips)—one per person, but should be different for each player per game

- List of supplies. Use the *Jump Back* Pioneers' List of Supplies as a guide or have groups make up their own. If creating a group list, provide paper and pencils.

TIPS FOR EXTRA FUN

- Winning players in each group receive a small prize (such as a gold spray-painted "nugget," first place ribbon, piece of candy).

- The entire rotating group can play one game together. In that case, every child receives a game board and they either take turns rolling the die and advancing along the board, or one person rolls one die and everyone advances together.

- As a group, decide what to bring on the journey—food, animals, clothing, tents, bedding. (Read "Pioneers' List of Supplies.") Discuss, if they could only bring one toy or memento, what would it be and why?

- When playing the game as a group, discuss conditions along the trail and find locations on the map. For example, when landing on "Fort Bridger—friends heading north on Oregon Trail," locate Fort Bridger and discuss where the trails separate and where each trail ends.

- Before playing the board game, have children trace the California and Oregon trails from Independence, Missouri. Discuss the importance of starting out late enough in the year so that grass was available for the animals, but early enough to pass over the mountains before winter storms. Discuss other difficulties faced by the pioneers.

- Discuss one day's walk (about 15 miles). Compare it to a round trip from home to school, for example, or from home to the next town. Try to imagine walking that distance over mountains, in thunderstorms, through dust kicked up by 100 wagons—every day for five months.

Pioneers' List of Supplies

What would a family of four need to carry in their wagon from Independence, Missouri, to California or Oregon? It's 2,000 miles, will take five months, and you'll have to fit everything into a wagon the size of a minivan. Don't forget your tent and your walking shoes! Your wagon is 10' × 3½' × 2' deep. Add 2,500 pounds of cargo:

- Food: 800 pounds flour; 500 pounds bacon or dried beef; 100 pounds coffee or tea; 200 pounds beans; 200 pounds lard; 100 pounds dried fruit; 200 pounds combined weight yeast, baking powder, vinegar, sugar, rice, salt, and pepper.

- 400 pounds of clothing, bedding, and tools. Include two sets of clothing per person and extra shoes (many people walked barefoot across the Sierra Nevada Mountains after their shoes wore out), bedding and tent (often a square of cloth over a pole with ropes and stakes. Some pioneers just threw a quilt on the ground, which was okay unless there were thunderstorms, stampedes, or wolves). Pioneers also brought tools, extra wagon axle, candles, matches, nails, pots, pans, utensils, buckets, butter churn, ax, guns, ammunition, axle grease, family heirlooms.

- Animals—horse, oxen, or mules. Some pioneers brought milk cows and chickens and herded them the whole 2,000 miles.

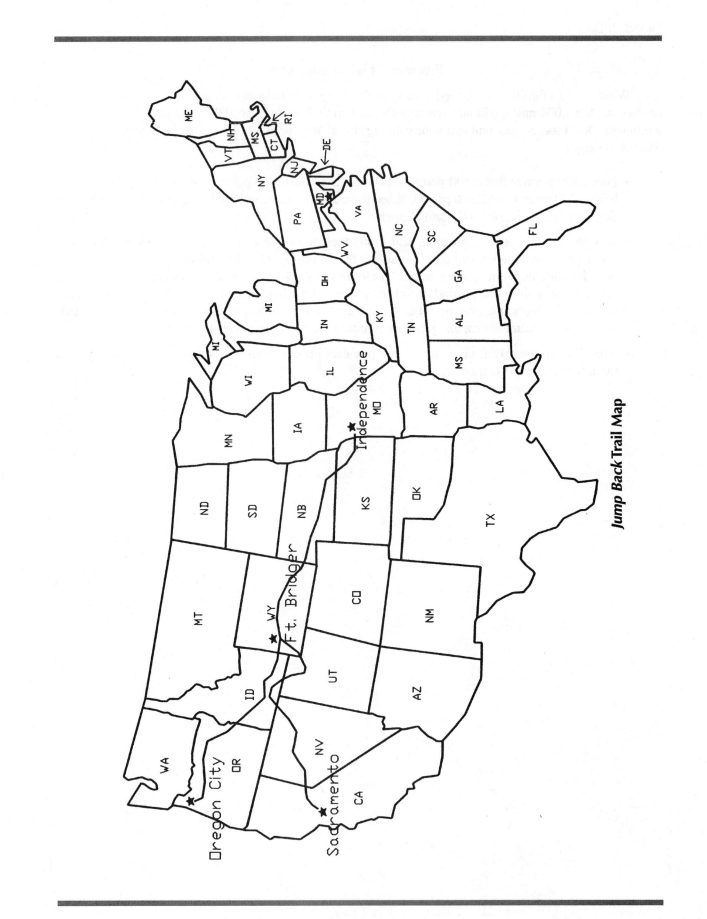

Jump Back **Trail Map**

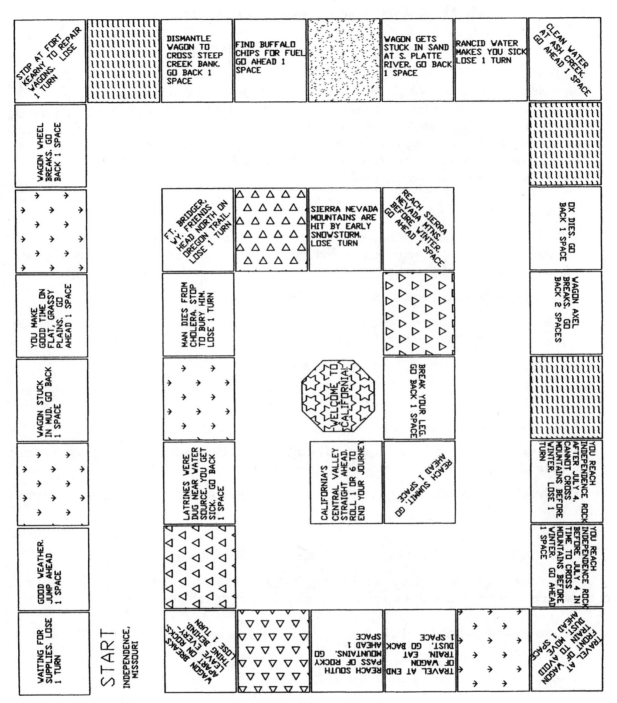

On the Trail Board Game

On the Trail can be played by two or more people. Each player rolls one die to move the game piece along the board. Players roll dice to decide who goes first—highest roll starts the game. Players follow instructions on the spaces they land on. Player must have exact roll to land on the last SQUARE. Players must then roll a "1" or "6" to reach California. First player to reach California wins.

HOME ON THE RANGE—LIFE IN THE OLD WEST

Station 4. Western Lasso and Rodeo Supply

At this station, children tie knots and learn how pioneers used them in everyday life. Have children sit on the floor (this activity works great outside) with a length of rope, a small box or book to tie up, and a pole (or they can practice tying the timber hitch onto their own leg). Pioneers used different knots for hunting, hitching animals to posts, hoisting things, anchoring heavy objects, and lashing poles together. Lead a discussion about how pioneers used ropes and knots in their daily lives and how we use them today. At this station you will need:

- Knot instructions

- Rope—enough lengths (approximately 3' each) for each child in the group. Tie a knot at one end of each rope; leave the other end frayed. All instructions use the terms "knotted end" and "frayed end."

- Small boxes or books for each child to tie the square knot

- Poles or broom handles for tying the timber hitch. If children are sitting on the floor, they can practice tying this knot on their own legs.

- Copy of "The Square Knot" for each child as handout

TIPS FOR EXTRA FUN

- See who can tie each knot fastest.

- List ways each knot could have been used by the pioneers. Make a different list of ways we could use each knot today.

- If there's time and this activity is being done outside, play the bullwhacker game (see instructions).

Bullwhacker Game (Play Outside)

Whips were used to urge oxen forward pulling the wagon. When the whip snapped, the loud crack in the air reminded the animals to keep moving. To play this game, you'll need:

- Rope—about 10' long (½" thick)

- 10" long stick with a flat top

- Coin

- Hammer

Poke (or hammer) the stick into the ground and balance the coin on top. Use the rope like a whip and try to knock the coin off without knocking the stick over. Make sure everybody stays far back from the rope!

The Square Knot

The square knot is the most common binding knot. It was used to tie up packages. Try tying a small box or book. Holding one end of rope in each hand, pass the frayed end over the knotted end, and tuck under.

Then make a loop with the knotted end so that it trails toward the right side.

Then pass the frayed end, which is now on the right bottom side, over the top knotted end, and tuck under. Pull both ends tight.

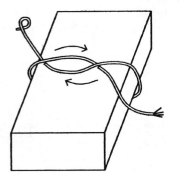 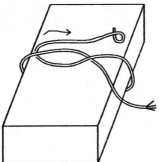 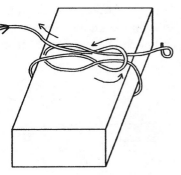

Square Knot

Timber Hitch

When pioneers reached the west, they had to haul logs to clear land and build houses. They tied a rope to the logs with a timber hitch knot and dragged them across the ground. The timber hitch tightens itself up when the rope is strained by the weight of a log. But when the rope is loose, the knot comes undone easily. That was important because tree branches and rough bark make it hard to untie knots. Let's try tying this knot around a pole or around our own legs while sitting on the ground.

Loop the frayed end of the rope up and over the side edge of your pole or leg. Leave the knotted end loose for dragging.

Bring the frayed end back up around the bottom of the pole and tuck it over and behind the knotted end.

Wind the frayed end around the diagonal part of the rope several times.

Pull on the knotted end of the rope. See how it holds the pole or your leg tight? Now let go of the rope and notice how the knot loosens.

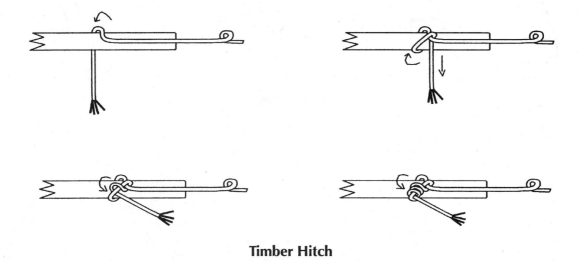

Timber Hitch

Farmer's Halter Loop

Pioneers used a farmer's halter loop to lead animals without choking them. To tie this knot, lay the rope on a flat surface and make a large loop. Turn the frayed end up and tuck it behind the large loop so it is now on the right side of the loop.

Tuck the frayed end back over the top of the large loop and through the small loop on the left side. Pull the knot tight.

The rope slips through the knot when you pull the knotted end, so an animal can move its neck without choking. Think about what kinds of animals the pioneers led using this knot.

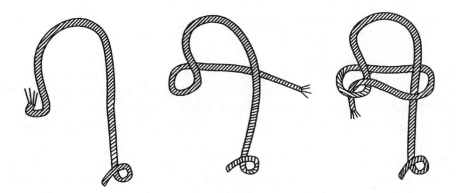

Halter Loop

Station 5. Better Butter Shop

Children make homemade butter at this station. You will need:

- These instructions
- Copy of "Pioneer Cooking along the Trail" for each child as handout
- Baby food-sized jars with lids (1 for every two children in each group—jars will be reused)
- Unwhipped whipping cream (the "milk" type in the carton; not already "whipped" cream). You will need ¼ cup for every two children
- Salt (optional)—one small "pinch" per jar
- ¼-cup measurer (The amount of cream used can be approximate, but measure so you don't run out of cream before all groups have made their butter.)
- Crackers (2–3 per child)
- Plastic knives for spreading butter
- Napkins or paper towels

Help children measure out ¼ cup heavy whipping cream into a baby-food sized jar. Add a pinch of salt. Allow one jar for two children. Make sure the lid is tight. Children take turns shaking their jar vigorously until the cream turns to butter. Spread butter on crackers.

While making butter, children may take turns reading the handout "Pioneer Cooking along the Trail" aloud (or an adult may read it aloud to the group). It's not necessary to completely clean the jars between groups unless they are sprinkled with cracker crumbs. Just add more cream and shake away!

TIPS FOR EXTRA FUN

- Discuss pioneer cooking along the trail: Children collected buffalo chips (dried buffalo poop) for campsite fuel. Everything was cooked outside even in the rain, dark, or dust. Imagine five months of eating bacon, hardtack, and dried fruit.
- Consider arranging station rotation so that tortillas are next—children can spread their homemade butter on warm tortillas.
- Sing a shaking song (one from the Music Hall). See who can shake the fastest. OR play follow the leader by shaking jars in circles, sideways, up and down, in unison.
- A marble in the jar speeds the churning process.

Pioneer Cooking Along the Trail

Main meals were breakfast and supper. Lunch was usually leftovers eaten during a noon rest stop. Hard tack (like thick, unsalted crackers), which could last for two years, was "fast food." When pioneers had time to make bread, the dough was often sprinkled with black specks—dead mosquitoes caught in the sticky dough. It was the kids' job to collect buffalo chips (dried buffalo poop) on the plains to burn as fuel for the campfire!

To make butter the old-fashioned way: Let fresh cow milk set for several hours so the cream floats to the top and turns sour. Put cream into a wooden bucket with a paddle (called a "churn") in the morning. The shaking of the wagon during the day will turn the cream to butter by nighttime. Ladle the butter off the top and into a bowl. Pour a little cold water into the butter and work it around with a paddle to wash the butter and keep it from going rancid (rotten). Keep doing this until the water stays clear when washed. Then mix in 1 teaspoon of salt per pound of butter. Press butter into a mold to get air bubbles out so people who buy it won't think you are cheating them.

MISSION MAKERS—SPANISH UNIT

Station 6. Old Adobe Cantina

Missions built throughout California by Roman Catholic priests brought Spanish culture to the West. Pioneers who settled in California learned many customs of everyday Spanish life. At this station, children make tortillas—flat, fried bread. Tortillas are sometimes filled with meat and cheese for a complete meal. But they are also good buttered, sprinkled with sugar, or just plain—hot off the griddle! At this station you will need (multiply ingredients by the number of recipes being made):

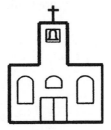

- These instructions
- 2 cups all-purpose flour
- 3 tablespoons shortening
- 1 teaspoon salt
- ½ cup warm water
- Measurers: 1 cup, ½ cup, tablespoon, teaspoon
- Large bowl
- Mixing spoon
- Knives or pastry cutter for cutting shortening into flour
- Spatula for turning tortillas
- Electric skillets—1 for every 3–4 students per group and extension cords if needed
- Napkins
- Optional butter, cinnamon sugar, shredded cheese, meat filling
- Access to soap, water, and towels for hand washing before and after cooking
- Copy of "Tasty Tortillas" for each child

Skillets should be heating as the first group arrives at this station. Children wash their hands and take turns adding ingredients and mixing the dough. Divide dough into one ball for each child. Children roll and flatten their own dough. Adult should be in charge of the skillets.

TIPS FOR EXTRA FUN

- Cinnamon sugar makes these homemade tortillas an extra treat! Mix cinnamon and sugar into a saltshaker for less mess.
- Have the butter station nearby and timed immediately before this station. Let children enjoy homemade butter on their warm tortillas.
- Although the recipe calls for the tortilla dough to sit for 10–15 minutes, it isn't absolutely necessary. Things go more smoothly, however, if the first batch of dough is made up before the first group arrives. Then, each group can make dough for the following group.
- Have access to soap, water, and towels before and after cooking. Have children handle only their own tortillas.

- Kids "count off" 1–4 for each skillet to help keep the location of their individual tortillas on the skillets straight, or they can put a drop of different food coloring on each tortilla.

- Discuss other Spanish foods that are part of American culture and foods from other cultures that are similar to tortillas (Greek pita bread, French crepes, Jewish blintzes, pancakes).

Tasty Tortillas

- 2 cups all-purpose flour
- 1 teaspoon salt
- 3 tablespoons shortening
- ½ cup warm water

Cut shortening into flour and salt until lumps are the size of small peas. Sprinkle in water, 1 tablespoon at a time, mixing until all flour is moistened and dough cleans sides of bowl. Gather dough into a ball; divide into 12 parts. Shape into balls. Cover and rest 10–15 minutes.

Pat each ball into a flat 6" circle. Heat nongreased skillet on medium-high heat. Cook tortilla until blisters appear on the surface (about 2 minutes). Turn over and cook the other side until dry (about 1 minute). Makes 12 tortillas.

Station 7. Senior Zapata's Toy Shop

At this station, children make piñatas—a papier-mâché toy later filled with candies or small prizes. Piñatas are typically hung at a party, where children take turns being blindfolded and hitting the piñata with a bat to break it open. Everyone shares the treats that fall to the ground. The piñata will need to dry overnight before it can be decorated and filled with treats. By using colored paper as the last layer, however, the body of these piñatas can be completed today. At this station you will need:

- These instructions

- One large round balloon (approximatly 9") for each piñata

- Papier-mâché (or flour)—4 cups per bowl

- 2 cups of warm water per bowl

- 1 large bowl or tub for every 3–4 children in the group

- Measuring cup for papier-mâché powder or flour

- Separate measuring cup for water

- Large mixing spoon

- Newspaper—ripped into strips approximately 1" × 4"

- Colored paper—ripped into strips approximately 1" × 4"

- Water, soap, and towels for cleanup

- Old shirts or aprons (this can get messy)

- Decorations—paint, paintbrushes, colored paper, yarn, glitter, glue, scissors

- Sharp knife to cut hole at top of piñata

- Wrapped candies or small toys

- Bat or long stick to break piñata

- Blindfold

- Wire (allow 6–8" for each piñata hook)

- Rope for hanging piñata

- Copies of "Say It in Spanish" for each child as handout

Mix papier-mâché or flour and water in a large bowl to a thin mixture—allow 3–4 children per bowl. Blow up balloon and tie end. Dip strips of newspaper into papier-mâché. Smooth off excess by running the strip through fingers. Place wet strip onto balloon and smooth down. Overlap strips until balloon is covered by 3–5 layers of paper. Apply a final layer of colored paper dipped in papier-mâché over the newspaper. Allow piñata to dry completely. Piñatas can be further decorated to create faces, animals (with dangly paper arms and legs), balls, and ornaments.

When dry, cut a 3-sided "hinged door" at the top of the piñata with a sharp knife. Fill with small candies or toys. Loop a wire through the top and hang piñata on a tree branch or basketball hoop with rope where it can swing freely. Children take turns being blindfolded (and traditionally spun 33 times to honor the 33 years that Jesus lived). Then the child is given a bat or long stick to hit the piñata. When the piñata breaks, all children share the treats.

TIPS FOR EXTRA FUN

- Do this outside, whether making or batting the piñata.

- Play Spanish background music.

- If this is for a classroom or scouting event, make the piñata at an earlier class or meeting. Then spend the time at this station decorating, filling, hanging, and batting it.

- Or purchase one inexpensive piñata per group and fill, hang, and bat them at this station. Make this station a party—a fiesta! Spend the time filling the piñata, practicing Spanish words, and then letting each blindfolded child take one or two swings.

- Or this station can be done as an end-of-the-day group activity. Hang one or more piñatas and celebrate together.

Say It in Spanish

People	la gente	weather	el tiempo
man	el hombre	rainy	iluvioso
woman	la mujer	snowy	nevado
boy	el chico	sunny	soleado
girl	la chica	it's hot	hace calor
children	los niños	it's cold	hace frío

fruit	las frutas	animals	los animals
apple	la manzana	dog	el perro
banana	el plátano	cat	el gato
lemon	el limon	pet	la mascota
tomato	el tomate	elephant	el elefante
orange	la naranja	wolf	el lobo
strawberry	la fresa	paw	la pata

GOLDEN LEGACY—CHINESE UNIT

Station 8. Wong's Diner

At this station, children use chopsticks to play a relay game and eat trail mix with chopsticks. You will need:

- These instructions
- One pair of chopsticks for each child to keep
- Four cotton balls
- 2 baskets, bowls, or boxes
- Small paper cups
- Trail mix (raisins, nuts, coconut, small candies mixed together)
- Large bowl to hold trail mix
- Copy of "I'm a Rat and You're a Pig" for each child as handout

Children each get a pair of chopsticks (they should not be reused) and form two lines—one line for each team. The first person in each line picks up a cotton ball with the chopsticks, runs to the other end of the room, and drops it into a basket. Then the child picks up a different cotton ball, runs back, and drops it in a basket at the front of the first line. The relay continues until everyone has played. The first team to complete the relay wins the game. After the relay, each child receives a small cup of trail mix to eat with chopsticks.

TIPS FOR EXTRA FUN

- Play the relay with other items—erasers, raisins, anything small but not too slippery.
- Discuss the advantages and disadvantages of chopsticks versus silverware.
- Use the chopsticks to eat the trail mix—don't cheat!
- Provide juice or water at this station as nuts and dried fruit make kids thirsty.

I'm a Rat and You're a Pig

Chinese legend says that Buddha invited all of the animals to join him for the New Year. He rewarded the animals who came by naming years after them. A person born in a year named for that animal shares the animals' qualities. The animals are the **RAT, OX, TIGER, RABBIT, DRAGON, SNAKE, HORSE, GOAT, MONKEY, ROOSTER, DOG,** and **PIG**. Find when you were born and see what animal you are associated with.

RAT

2/2/1984 TO 2/19/1985

2/19/1996 TO 2/6/1997

OX (or BUFFALO)

2/20/1985 TO 2/8/1986

2/7/1985 TO 2/8/1986

TIGER

2/9/1986 TO 1/28/1987

1/28/1998 TO 2/15/1999

RABBIT (or CAT)

1/29/1987 TO 2/16/1988

2/16/1999 TO 2/4/2000

DRAGON

2/17/1988 TO 2/5/1989

2/5/2000 TO 1/23/2001

SNAKE

2/6/1989 TO 1/26/1990

1/24/2001 TO 2/11/2002

HORSE

1/27/1990 TO 2/14/1991

2/12/2002 TO 1/31/2003

GOAT

2/15/1991 TO 2/3/1992

2/01/2003 TO 1/21/2004

MONKEY

2/16/1980 TO 2/4/1981

2/4/1992 TO 1/22/1993

ROOSTER

1/22/2004 TO 2/08/2005

2/9/2005 TO 1/28/2006

DOG

2/10/1994 TO 1/30/1995

1/29/2006 TO 2/17/2007

PIG

2/13/1983 TO 2/1/1984

1/31/1995 TO 2/18/1996

Station 9. Beaded Calculators

Building a Chinese abacus is a fun way to practice math! At this station you will need:

- These instructions
- Copy of "Abacus ABCs" for each child as handout
- One 6" × 12" piece of lightweight cardboard or poster board for each abacus
- 50 beads of one color with large center holes (blue for our example) for each abacus
- 20 beads of another color (yellow for our example) for each abacus
- String that fits through the bead holes
- Scissors, markers, rulers

Using a ruler and marker, draw three horizontal lines across the cardboard: 1" down from the top edge; 2" down from the top edge; and 1" up from the bottom edge.

Cut ten slits at the top of the cardboard from the edge to the top line, spaced 1" apart. Cut ten corresponding slits at the bottom edge, spaced 1" apart.

With a felt pen, number the bottom slits "1–10" from right to left.

Write a "1" below the middle line and a "5" above the center line.

Cut 10 pieces of 14" string. Insert one end of string into the first top slit (number 1). Slide 2 yellow beads onto the string and then 5 blue beads. Stretch the string down to the bottom slit, pull it snug, and tie at the back of the cardboard. Repeat so all rows hold a string with 2 yellow beads at the top of the abacus and 5 blue beads at the bottom.

TIPS FOR EXTRA FUN

- Solve addition and subtraction problems. Enter the beginning number on the abacus and then add or subtract beads.
- You can adjust instructions and make a smaller abacus with fewer rows of beads.
- These instructions have been simplified using blue and yellow beads, but any two colors of beads can be used.

Abacus ABCs

The middle horizontal line is called the "beam." The part of the abacus above the beam is the "upper deck." The part of the abacus below the beam is the "lower deck."

Starting from the right, the row of beads at slit number 1 is the ones column. The next row of beads is the tens column. The next row is the hundreds column, then thousands, and so on.

Each blue bead is one unit. For example, each blue bead in row number 1 equals 1; each blue bead in row number 2 equals 10; each blue bead in row number 3 equals 100, and so on. Each yellow bead counts as 5 units. For example, each yellow bead in row number 1 equals 5; each yellow bead in row number 2 equals 50, and so on. Start by placing the blue beads toward the bottom line and the yellow beads toward the top line. You count by moving beads toward the beam. Let's make the number 105,637:

Move 2 blue beads and 1 yellow bead toward the beam in the row number 1 (to show the number 7), leaving the rest where they were.

Move 3 blue beads toward the beam in row number 2 (to show the number 30).

Move 1 blue bead and 1 yellow bead toward the beam in row number 3 (to show the number 600).

Move 1 yellow bead toward the beam in row number 4 (to show the number 5,000).

Don't move any beads in row number 5 but move 1 blue bead toward the beam in row number 6 (to show the number 10,000).

Unused beads in all remaining columns are pushed toward the edges.

Try solving addition and subtraction problems using the abacus. To do this, enter the beginning number on the abacus and then add or subtract beads to equal the second number.

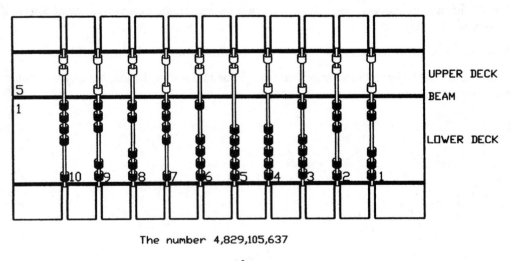

The number 4,829,105,637

Abacus

HUNTERS AND GATHERERS—NATIVE AMERICAN UNIT

Station 10. Chumash Bank

At this station, children learn about the Chumash tribe in southern California and their use of shell beads as money. Read aloud the handout "Painters and Bankers." At this station you will need:

- These instructions

- Copy of "Painters and Bankers" for each child to read aloud

- Dried macaroni noodles

- String, twine, or yarn cut in 3' lengths

- Scissors

- Tape

- Colored markers

Children decorate dried macaroni noodles (allow 20–30 per child) with markers (paint may leave noodles limp) in solid colors, dots, stripes, or other designs. They are making "money," so have them decide what each decoration will mean. For example, one solid red noodle could equal 5 blue striped noodles; one blue striped noodle equals 10 green dotted noodles.

Cut a length of string approximately 3'. Tape one end of the string. Thread beads and tie ends together to wear as a necklace. After everyone has decorated their money have them share the monetary system they invented.

TIPS FOR EXTRA FUN

- Discuss other things people could use for money—shiny rocks, carved wood, food.

- Compare our use of paper money and Chumash shell beads (they wore their money; no need for pockets; paper is destroyed easily).

- Have everyone make the same kind and number of beads. For example, have everyone make 5 red beads, 5 blue striped beads, and 10 green dotted beads. Then have an auction for small prizes with the winner "paying" for his prize with some of the beads.

Painters and Bankers

The Chumash people are known for cave paintings and for shell bead money. Some of the cave paintings, thought to show religious ideas or mythical figures, can still be seen in southern California. Paints were made from minerals—red from iron oxide, white from gypsum, black from charcoal. The minerals were mixed with water, animal fat, or plant juice and painted onto rock walls with fingers or brushes made from animal tails.

Today we use circles of metal and pieces of paper for money. The Chumash used beads. Beads were cut into discs from a purple ocean snail shell, called the olivella (ah-li-VEL-a). The Chumash cut a hole in the center, threaded the disks onto string, and wore them as necklaces. The part of the shell each bead was made from determined what each bead was worth. For example, several beads could be made from the wall of the shell, so those were less valuable than beads made from the thick opening.

The Chumash would determine the value of a strand of shell beads by how many times it could be wrapped around a person's hand. Because the disk beads were very small, it took a lot of beads to make one necklace.

Station 11. Miwok Village

Children at this station will play "shinny," a game similar to our golf and hockey. This game trained Miwoks in hunting skills by teaching spear handling. At this station you will need:

- These instructions

- Baseball bats or long poles (such as broom handles)—1 for each player

- A ball—baseball size or smaller

- 4 sticks for the goals

- Copy of "Miwok Talk" for each child as handout

This game should be played outside on a large field. Divide children into two teams. Poke 2 sticks into the ground about 2' apart at each end of the field for "goals." Each team tries to hit the ball between the stakes of the other team using the poles. Each goal is one point. The team with the most points at the end of the time wins.

TIPS FOR EXTRA FUN

- Use Miwok names for each team (see handout).

- To play a relay, only 2 poles and balls are needed. Teams form two lines and try to control the ball with the pole across a line and back. The team that finishes first wins.

- Winning team members beat a "drum" (decorated box) or do a celebration "dance."

Miwok Talk

Boy:	**NANYA TIE**
Girl:	**OHSA TIE**
Yes:	**HOO**
No:	**EH-WOO-TOO**
Earth (World):	**WALL-LIE**
Sun:	**HIGH-YE-MA**
Moon:	**KO-MAY**
Mosquito:	**OO-YOO-KOO-SOO**
Deer:	**OO-WYU-YA**
Grizzly Bear:	**OOSOO-MA-TIE**

(possibly the origin of the word "Yosemite")

A NEW WAY TO GO—RAILROADS

Station 12. Railroad Station

At this station, children learn about the building of the transcontinental railroad and how it helped unite the early West with the rest of America. First introduce the map of the United States and trace the transcontinental railroad from both directions—the section built by the Union Pacific Railroad Company westward from Omaha, Nebraska, and the section built by the Central Pacific Railroad Company eastward from Sacramento, California, using *Jump Back* Map of Transcontinental Railroad as a guide. Discuss building a railroad through the Sierra Nevada, the Rocky Mountains, the plains, and the desert without modern equipment. Read aloud the handout "The Long Metal Road." Pass out one board game for every two children. At this station you will need:

- These instructions

- Copy of Roads from Rails board game, enlarged as needed—1 for every 2 children (laminated copies last longer)

- One die for every 2 children

- Game pieces (buttons, paperclips, slips of paper, dried beans); should be different for each player per game

- Large map of U.S. (optional)

- Copy of *Jump Back* Map of Transcontinental Railroad

- Copy of "The Long Metal Road" for each child as handout

- Candy or small prizes for winning teams, if desired

The Roads from Rails board game can be played by two people or in teams. Divide the children into groups with board game and 1 die for each group and 1 game piece per player. One player, representing the Central Pacific Railroad Company, starts at Sacramento, California, and builds the railroad eastward. The other player, representing the Union Pacific Railroad Company, starts at Omaha, Nebraska, and builds the railroad westward. The first to reach Promontory Point, Utah, wins.

Each player rolls one die to decide who goes first—the highest roll starts the game. Players roll die to move their game pieces along the board, following the instructions on the spaces where they land. Players must have an exact roll of the die to land on the last SQUARE. The player must then roll either a "1" or a "6" to reach Promontory Point, Utah.

TIPS FOR EXTRA FUN

- Play the game as teams. Give each child a copy of the game board, but divide each group into 2— one team playing for the Central Pacific Railroad Company; the other team playing for the Union Pacific Railroad Company. The team to reach Promontory Point, Utah, first wins.

- The winning person or team receives a candy or small prize.

- Discuss the notes on the game spaces.

- Discuss which railroad children would have rather worked for—and why.

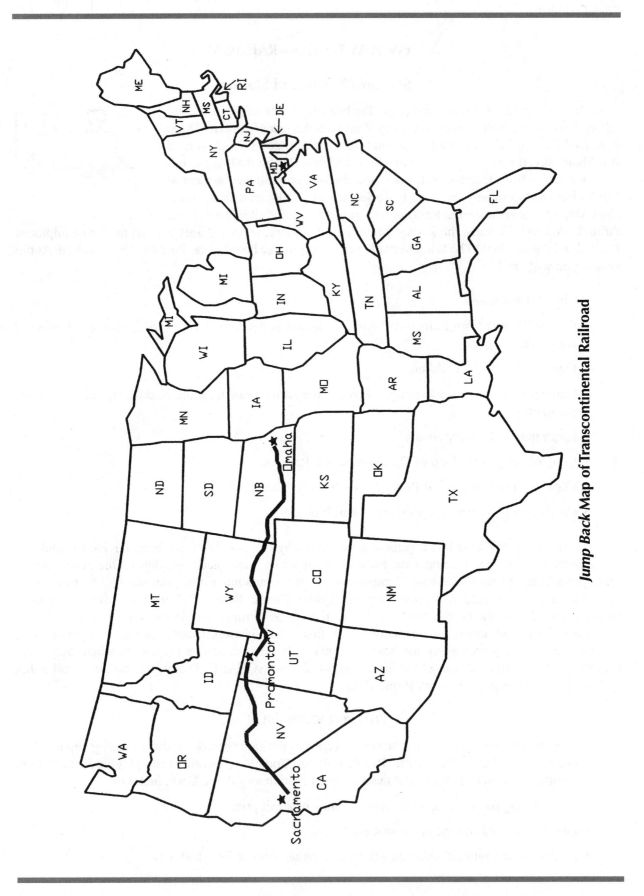

Jump Back Map of Transcontinental Railroad

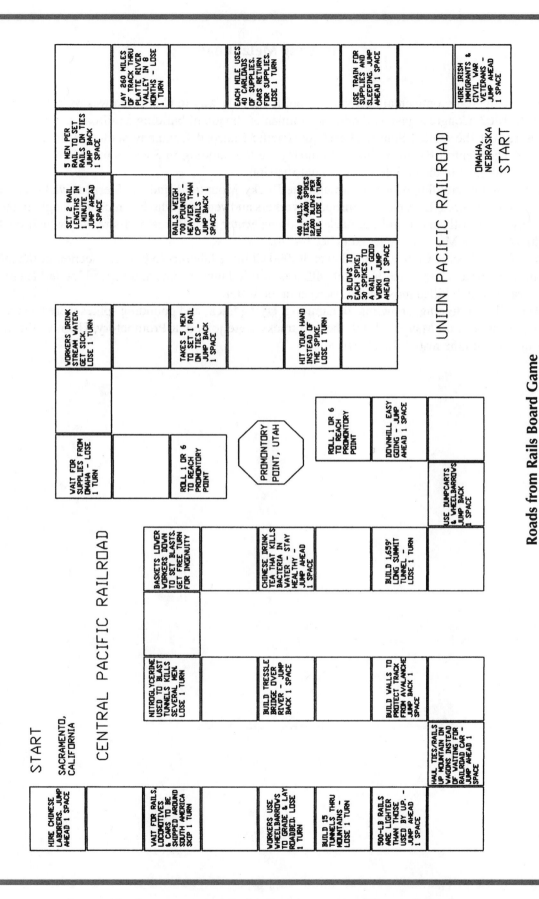

Roads from Rails Board Game

The board game contains the following spaces:

UNION PACIFIC RAILROAD

START — OMAHA, NEBRASKA

- HIRE IRISH IMMIGRANTS & CIVIL WAR VETERANS – JUMP AHEAD 1 SPACE
- USE TRAIN FOR SUPPLIES AND SLEEPING. JUMP AHEAD 1 SPACE
- EACH MILE USES 40 CARLOADS OF SUPPLIES. CARS RETURN FOR SUPPLIES. LOSE 1 TURN
- LAY 260 MILES OF TRACK THRU PLATTE RIVER VALLEY IN 8 MONTHS – LOSE 1 TURN
- 5 MEN PER RAIL TO SET RAILS ON TIES – JUMP BACK 1 SPACE
- SET 2 RAIL LENGTHS IN 1 MINUTE – JUMP AHEAD 1 SPACE
- RAILS WEIGH 700 POUNDS – HEAVIER THAN CP RAILS – JUMP BACK 1 SPACE
- 400 RAILS, 2400 TIES, 4,000 SPIKES 12,000 BLOWS PER MILE. LOSE 1 TURN
- WORKERS DRINK STREAM WATER. GET SICK. LOSE 1 TURN
- TAKES 5 MEN TO SET 1 RAIL ON TIES – JUMP BACK 1 SPACE
- HIT YOUR HAND INSTEAD OF THE SPIKE. LOSE 1 TURN
- 3 BLOWS TO EACH SPIKE, 30 SPIKES TO A RAIL – GOOD WORK! JUMP AHEAD 1 SPACE
- WAIT FOR SUPPLIES FROM OMAHA – LOSE 1 TURN
- ROLL 1 OR 6 TO REACH PROMONTORY POINT
- ROLL 1 OR 6 TO REACH PROMONTORY POINT
- DOWNHILL EASY GOING – JUMP AHEAD 1 SPACE
- USE DUMPCARTS & WHEELBARROWS JUMP BACK 1 SPACE

PROMONTORY POINT, UTAH

CENTRAL PACIFIC RAILROAD

START — SACRAMENTO, CALIFORNIA

- HIRE CHINESE LABORERS. JUMP AHEAD 1 SPACE
- WAIT FOR RAILS, LOCOMOTIVES & CARS TO BE SHIPPED AROUND SOUTH AMERICA SKIP 1 TURN
- WORKERS USE WHEELBARROWS TO GRADE & LAY ROADBED. LOSE 1 TURN
- BUILD 15 TUNNELS THRU MOUNTAINS – LOSE 1 TURN
- 500-LB RAILS ARE LIGHTER THAN THOSE USED BY UP. – JUMP AHEAD 1 SPACE
- HAUL TIES/RAILS UP MOUNTAIN ON WAGONS INSTEAD OF WAITING FOR RAILROAD CAR – JUMP AHEAD 1 SPACE
- NITROGLYCERINE USED TO BLAST TUNNELS KILLS SEVERAL MEN LOSE 1 TURN
- BASKETS LOWER WORKERS DOWN TO SET BLASTS. GET FREE TURN FOR INGENUITY
- BUILD TRESSLE BRIDGE OVER RIVER – JUMP BACK 1 SPACE
- CHINESE DRINK TEA THAT KILLS BACTERIA IN WATER – STAY HEALTHY – JUMP AHEAD 1 SPACE
- BUILD WALLS TO PROTECT TRACK FROM AVALANCHE JUMP BACK 1 SPACE
- BUILD 1,659' LONG SUMMIT TUNNEL – LOSE 1 TURN

The Long Metal Road

Before the transcontinental railroad was built, the only way to California was by horse, wagon, or on foot. In 1862, Congress gave two railroad companies the job of building a railroad to unite California with the rest of the United States. The Union Pacific Railroad Company started building in Omaha, Nebraska. The Central Pacific Railroad Company started building in Sacramento, California. The two tracks were to meet in the middle—at Promontory, Utah.

It was tough building over and through the Rocky Mountains and the Sierra Nevada. The Union Pacific Company hired thousands of European workers and veterans who had recently fought in the Civil War. They ate mostly meat and hardtack and drank water from lakes and streams, which contained unhealthy bacteria. Many of the workers became ill.

The Union Pacific Company hired over 30,000 Chinese laborers to build its section of the railroad. The Chinese workers had a healthier diet with lots of dried mushrooms and vegetables and tea made by boiling water, which killed most of the bacteria in the water.

The miles of digging, tunneling, dynamiting, laying track, and pounding spikes were backbreaking and dangerous. But on May 10, 1869, the two tracks were joined at Promontory, Utah. California was finally united with the rest of the United States!

Station 13. Telegraph Company

At this station, children learn about how the telegraph affected westward migration. They will practice sending and receiving coded messages either using pencils and paper to "send" code or by using a homemade telegraph machine. At this station you will need:

- These instructions

- Pencils and paper

- Copies of "Morse Coded Sample Messages"

- Copy of "Decoding Dots and Dashes" for each child as handout

- Copy of "Sam's Marvelous Machine" to read aloud (and hand out, if desired)

- Homemade telegraph (optional but definitely more fun)

Have children take turns reading "Sam's Marvelous Machine" aloud. Then have them practice writing out messages with pencil and paper using Morse code. Exchange messages and try to decode them. If a homemade telegraph has been made, explain how it is used and let children take turns "sending" messages.

TIPS FOR EXTRA FUN

- Give the group a written message to decode. The first to decode it wins a prize.

- Have children transcribe their names into Morse code.

- Have children tap or clap out Morse code—quick tap/clap for dots; tap/clap followed by a pause for dashes. Discuss how telegraph operators first used a pencil and paper to write down the dots and dashes and later learned to "hear" the code.

- Make a homemade telegraph prior to the event (see page 171). Let kids practice sending messages and listening to the distinctive "clicking" sounds of Morse code.

- Construct a telegraph beforehand as a class science or scout project. Discuss how electricity along the circuit creates a magnet to pull the metal "T" down to tap against the nail.

Sam's Marvelous Machine

Early in history, it was hard to send messages long distance. People had to deliver messages in person or use signals. If they could see each other, they could use fire or flags to send messages. If they could hear each other, they could use drums or church bells. After electricity was discovered, a switch on a machine could send short pulses of electric current along a wire. That machine was called a telegraph.

In 1831, Samuel F. B. Morse created a new telegraph receiver with an iron arm to catch the electric currents. The electric pulses made the arm "bounce." So he attached a pencil to the arm and rested it against a moving strip of paper. When the arm bounced, the pencil made marks on the paper. Depending on how long the electric pulse ran through the wire, the pencil would either make short dots or long dashes on the paper. Later, Morse created a code using the short and long pulses to represent letters and numbers. Morse code could be understood so easily by its "clicking" that telegraph operators eventually stopped using the paper and pencil and just listened to the sounds.

The telegraph became an important way to send messages quickly over the long distances in the early West. Since railroads linked towns, railroad and telegraph companies cooperated. The railroad companies laid telegraph lines along its tracks and provided space inside train stations for telegraph operators. In return, the telegraph company sent messages for the railroad free of charge and gave priority to messages about train movements. Since the railroad company could know the exact location of trains, trains could move more quickly and safely.

PACK YOUR WAGON

• — — •   • —   — • — •   — • —

— • — —   — — —   • • —   • — •

• — —   • — —   — — •   — — — •   — •

GO WEST

— — •   — — —

• — —   •   • • •   —

OUR SECRET

— — —   • • —   • — •

• • •   •   — • — •   • — •   •   —

Morse Coded Sample Messages

Decoding Dots and Dashes

In the 1800s, people began to communicate by sending electric currents along a wire. Samuel Morse created a telegraph receiver that caused these electric pulses to make marks on a strip of paper. The marks looked like dots when the pulses were short and like dashes when the pulses were long. His "Morse code" used these short and long pulses to represent letters and numbers. You can use Morse code to send secret messages to your friends!

A . _	B _ . . .	C _ . _ .
D _ . .	E .	F . . _ .
G _ _ .	H	I . .
J . _ _ _	K _ . _	L . _ . .
M _ _	N _ .	O _ _ _
P . _ _ .	Q _ _ . _	R . _ .
S . . .	T _	U . . _
V . . . _	W . _ _	X _ . . _
Y _ . _ _	Z _ _ . .	1 . _ _ _ _
2 . . _ _ _	3 . . . _ _	4 . . . . _
5	6 _	7 _ _ . . .
8 _ _ _ . .	9 _ _ _ _ .	0 _ _ _ _ _
PERIOD . _ . _ . _	COMMA _ _ . . _ _	? . . _ _ . .

HOW TO MAKE A HOMEMADE TELEGRAPH

A simple telegraph consists of a key, a sounder (which makes the buzzing sound), and a battery. To make a telegraph you will need:

- Flat piece of wood (approximately 6" × 8" × 1" thick)
- 2 wood blocks (approximately 2" × 3" × ¾" thick)
- 5 steel nails (long enough to go through one block and into the flat piece of wood)
- 1 aluminum nail
- 3 metal thumbtacks
- 1 T-shaped piece of flexible steel
- 1 thin strip of metal (brass, copper, or steel)
- Insulated wire (approximately 3')
- Number 6 battery

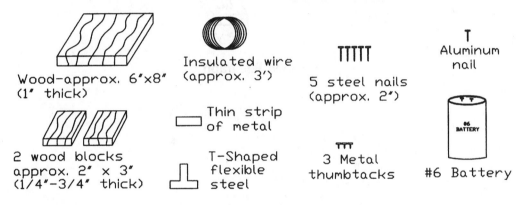

Wood-approx. 6"x8" (1" thick)

Insulated wire (approx. 3')

5 steel nails (approx. 2")

Aluminum nail

2 wood blocks approx. 2" × 3" (1/4"–3/4" thick)

Thin strip of metal

T-Shaped flexible steel

3 Metal thumbtacks

#6 Battery

Homemade Telegraph Items Needed

Nail one small block of wood onto the large wood base using 2 steel nails. Attach the T-shaped metal to the end of the block with a 3rd nail, as shown. Hammer two steel nails into one end of the base, so that approximately 1" of both nails is above the top of the wood.

Wind a piece of insulated wire around each of the 2 nails about 30 times to form coils. Leave 1 wire end loose to connect to the battery and the other wire end loose to connect to the key.

Hammer the aluminum nail just in front of the T-shaped metal and bend it over the top of the T so that the head of the nail touches the T.

To make the key—press 2 thumbtacks halfway through the thin metal strip into the 2nd block of wood. Strip the insulation from approximately 1" of the end of one wire coming from the sounder coil and wrap the bare wire around the tacks. Press the tacks down firmly into the thin metal and wood block.

Pressing down firmly on the 2 thumbtacks, bend the back end of the thin metal key upward so that it is raised about ½" from the surface of the wood block. When you press the key, the metal should touch the tack and spring back when released. Press the 3rd thumbtack halfway into the wood underneath the raised part of the key at the back of the block.

Cut a length of wire about 12" long. Strip the insulation from 1" of the end and wrap the bare wire around the 3rd tack. Press the tack firmly into the wooden block. Strip the insulation from 1" of the other end of the 12" wire and attach the bare wire to one terminal of the battery. Strip and attach the 2nd wire from the coils on the sounder to the 2nd terminal of the battery in the same way.

Once both wires are attached to the battery, when the key is pressed, the thin metal will touch the tack. This causes an electric current to flow through the circuit, forming an electromagnet that pulls the metal T down, making a clicking sound. When the key is released, the magnet is broken. The T is released and strikes the bent nail at the top, making another clicking sound. These sounds represent the dots and dashes of Morse code.

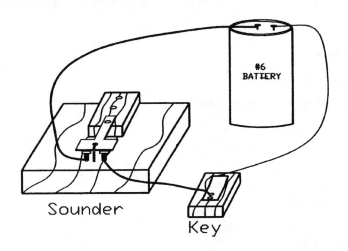

Finished Telegraph

END THE DAY AS A GROUP

Station 14. Photography Palace and Print Shop

Group photographs are combined with assembling the souvenir booklet for this end-of-the-day activity. Gather each group in front of the mural made at the Blacksmith Shop, have them pose, and snap their picture! While photographs are being taken, children put together their souvenir booklets (see Chapter 1). At this station you will need:

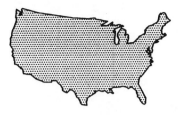

- The community mural(s) made at the Blacksmith Shop

- Tape or tacks to attach mural to wall (or children can hold smaller poster board murals)

- Camera and film

- Optional costumes and/or props

- Colored construction paper

- Stapler

- Crayons, colored markers

TIPS FOR EXTRA FUN

- The more elaborate the costumes and props—the more the fun!

- Have Old West music playing in the background

- Make copies of the photo for everybody

- SMILE!

Appendix 1

Sample Rotation Schedule

WHAT HAPPENS	TIMING
Adults arrive/set up	8:00–8:30
Start the day as a group	8:30–9:00
Rotation to next station	9:00–9:05
Activity	9:05–9:20
Rotation to next station	9:20–9:25
Activity	9:25–9:40
Recess (adjust timing; nonschool event add activity here)	9:40–9:55
Rotation to next station	9:55–10:00
Activity	10:00–10:15
Rotation to next station	10:15–10:20
Activity	10:20–10:35
Rotation to next station	10:35–10:40
Activity	10:40–10:55
Rotation to next station	10:55–11:00
Activity	11:00–11:15
Rotation to next station	11:15–11:20
Activity	11:20–11:35
Rotation (if a nonschool activity; for schools—regroup for lunch dismissal)	11:35–11:40
Lunch (adjust timing) nonschool events can have two activities and rotations during this time	11:40–12:30
Activity	12:30–12:45
Rotation to next station	12:45 –12:50
Activity	12:50–1:05
Rotation to next station	1:05–1:10
Activity	1:10–1:25
Recess (adjust to fit timing; for nonschool event add activity)	1:25–1:40

WHAT HAPPENS	TIMING
Rotation to next station	1:40–1:45
Activity	1:45–2:00
Rotation to next station	2:00–2:05
Activity	2:05–2:20
Rotation to next station	2:20–2:25
End the day as a group	2:25–2:45
Cleanup	2:45–3:15

Master Volunteer Schedule

(Use 1 list for each station; 1 for timekeeper; 1 for set up/cleanup)

STATION: _____ LOCATION:_____

ACTIVITY:_____

Volunteer Name	Time
_____	_____
_____	_____
_____	_____
_____	_____
_____	_____

STATION: _____ LOCATION:_____

ACTIVITY:_____

Volunteer Name	Time
_____	_____
_____	_____
_____	_____
_____	_____
_____	_____

TIME KEEPER

LOCATION: Roaming

This person will be responsible for getting kids to move from one station to another; will keep a stopwatch and use bullhorn to announce station moves.

Volunteer Name	Time
_____	_____
_____	_____

SET UP/CLEANUP

LOCATION: All stations

Volunteers to help with set up and cleanup.

Volunteer Name	Time
_____	_____
_____	_____
_____	_____
_____	_____
_____	_____
_____	_____

Appendix 3

Letter to Parents

JUMP BACK IN TIME!

On _____ (date), we're going to jump back in time and celebrate history with _____ (name of event). Kids will experience life and culture as it used to be with hands-on activities, games, food, and fun.

We need some "time travelers" to help with this fun-filled day of activities. If you're available to help for part or all of the day, to lead small groups of kids through hands-on learning activities (instructions provided), please call _____ (contact name) at _____ (phone number).

If you are able to donate supplies, following is a list of items needed. We'll let you know when those things are needed.

Thanks for your help. We're looking forward to a fun day of learning!

(Attach list of items needed for donations)

Reminder Notice to Volunteers

JUMP BACK IN TIME!

_____ (name of event) will blow into town on _____! If you've agreed to help at the event or send in items, we're counting on you! It's going to be a hoot, so we'd like to extend one last invitation to helpers. Even if you can only help for a few hours, we'd love you to join the fun.

We'll be "going back in time," so kids and helpers, dress up and get into the mood. Remember—early history involved many peoples and cultures. So pull out those costumes and get creative.

Questions? Call _____ at _____.

Notice Confirming Volunteers

To: _____ (adult name)

Thank you for volunteering to join the fun at our living history event!

This event will be set up with _____ "stations" to teach history through games, crafts, and other activities. The children will rotate through stations in small groups, spending between 10–15 minutes at each station before rotating to the next.

You are scheduled to work at the _____ station on _____ (date) for the following time period _____.

If you have any questions, please phone _____ (name of contact) at _____.

Everyone is encouraged to wear costumes to add to the fun and get everyone in the mood! Thanks for your help.

Glossary

ANCIENT CULTURES DAY

ATHENA (a-THEE-na)—Greek goddess of wisdom, art, and war

BUL—Mayan game similar to checkers

CALLIGRAPHY (cah-LIG-ra-fee)—a form of Chinese writing, which means "good writing"

CARTOUCHE (car-TOOSH)—frame placed around names of Egyptian kings, queens, and gods

CUNEIFORM (que-NA-eh-form)—ancient writing on wet clay from Mesopotamia

GREGORIAN CALENDAR—created by Pope Gregory XIII in 1582 and used today

HAMMURABI (ha-mur-Ah-bee)—King of Babylon about 1700 B.C.

HATHOR (HA-thor)—Egyptian goddess of love and family

HEBREW (HE-bru)—language used by the ancient Israel culture

HIEROGLYPHICS (high-row-GLIF-ix)—picture writing used by ancient Egyptians

HUNAHPU (hoo-nah-POOH)—Mayan twin who fought gods of death in the underworld

ILLUYANKAS (Il-oo-YAN-kus)—Hittite storm god

INARAS (Ih-NAR-us)—Hittite goddess of wild animals (daughter of Illuyankas)

JULIAN CALENDAR—named after Julius Caesar (SEE-zar) Emperor of Rome about 46 B.C.

KING DAVID—shepherd, musician, and king of Israel about 1100 B.C., and ancestor of Jesus Christ

LYRE—musical stringed instrument used throughout many ancient cultures

MAYANS (MY-ans)—ancient culture living in Mesoamerica

MT. OLYMPUS (oh-LIM-pus)—mountain where ancient Greeks believed the gods lived

OLD TESTAMENT (TEST-a-ment)—religious writings from the Torah in the Christian Bible

OWARE (oh-WAH-re)—ancient Egyptian board game

PHARAOHS (feh-ROWS)—ancient Egyptian kings

POISEIDON (po-SIGH-don)—Greek god of the sea

POMPILIUS (pom-PILL-e-us)—Emperor of Rome about 715 B.C.

POPUL-VUH (POH-pole VOO)—Sixteenth-century book containing ancient Mayan stories

QIN SHI HUANG (CHIN SHEE WAN)—China's first Emperor

QUETZALCOATL (quat-zal-COAT-al)—Mayan god believed to return one day

RA—Egyptian sun god

ROMAN NUMERALS—numbering system used by ancient Romans, using only 7 symbols

ROMULUS (RAH-mew-lus) and REMUS (REE-mus)—mythical brothers who founded Rome

ROSETTA STONE—stone tablet that enabled people to read Egyptian hieroglyphics

SHU (shoo)—Egyptian god of air, son of Ra

TEFNUT (TEF-nut)—Egyptian goddess of moisture, daughter of RA

TORAH (TOR-ah)—religious writings of the Jewish people

XBALANQUE (sh-bah-LAHN-kay)—Mayan twin who fought gods of death in the underworld

NATIVE AMERICA DAY

ADOBE (ah-DOH-be)—mixture of mud and grass used in the southwest to cover buildings

AGAVE (a-GAV-ee)—wild plant eaten by tribes in the Southwestern region

CHIEF JOSEPH—Nez Percé chief known for his military leadership and hope for justice

CHILKAT (CHILL-cat) BLANKETS—5-sided Tlinget blankets worn as capes

COYOTE—a creature in legend, sometimes a trickster, sometimes wise, who helped humans

ESKIMOS (ES-ki-moz)—name given to Inuit people by other tribes, means "raw fish eaters"

FRONTLETS—carved wooden headdresses worn by nobles on the northwestern coast

HOGANS—5-sided domed Navajo home framed with wood and covered in clay

HOLE-IN-THE-DAY—Ojibway leader

KACHINAS (ka-CHI-nas)—helpful spirits of the Hopi culture

MANIILAQ (MAN-ih-lak), THE PROPHET—Inuit leader known for his spiritual predictions

MUKLUK (MUK-luck)—seal or reindeer skin boot worn by Eskimos

NAVAJO CODE TALKERS—Marines in World War II who used Navajo language for secret codes

PARFLECHE (PAR-flesh)—bag used to hold food and small items when traveling

POTLATCH (POT-lach)—multiday feasts in the northwest region

PUEBLO (poo-EB-low)—type of house of clay or stones, also refers to certain southwest people

RAVEN—popular creature in legends who aided humans

SEATTLE (see-AT-el)—chief of Suquamish and Duwamish tribes

SEQUOYAH (seh-COY-ah)—created written symbols of Cherokee language

SITTING BULL—Sioux chief who defeated General Custer at the Battle of Little Bighorn

SPIDER WOMAN—mythical creature who helped humans, including bringing sun to the world

WIKIUP (WI-kee-up)—southwestern housing made by covering poles with grass or brush

COLONIAL AMERICA DAY

CALVERT, Sir George—began the colony of Maryland for Roman Catholics

DE LA WARR, Lord—brought supplies and settlers to America; Delaware was named after him

GRANVILLE, Lord—last of eight English gentlemen who held title to the land of North Carolina

HUTCHINSON, Anne—Rhode Island settler, believed women had a right to speak at church

HORNBOOKS—wooden board covered in clear animal horn used in schools to practice writing

INDIGO (IN-dih-go)—plant used to make a deep blue dye for coloring fabric

JOHNNY CAKES—flat, fried bread

LIMNERS—traveling artists who used prepainted canvases into which new faces were added

LUCAS, Elizabeth "Eliza"—developed indigo as an important crop for the southern colonies

OGLETHORPE, James Edward—British general started colony of Georgia as a place for debtors

PENN, William—founded the colony of Pennsylvania for Quakers to practice their religion

PILGRIMS—the first people to come to America to settle there permanently

QUILLING—art form using curled paper strips

QUOITS (kwaits)—game similar to horseshoes

SMITH, Captain John—one of the leaders of the Jamestown settlement

STUYVESANT, Peter—Dutch governor who surrendered to the Duke of York

TALLOW (TAL-low)—animal fat used to make candles

TRUMBULL, Jonathan—British governor of Connecticut who supported American independence

WHEELWRIGHT, Reverend John—began settlement of Exeter, New Hampshire

WILLIAMS, Roger—kicked out of Massachusetts by Puritans, founded Providence, Rhode Island

PIONEER DAY

ABACUS—ancient counting board using beads

CENTRAL PACIFIC RAILROAD—built transcontinental railroad east from Sacramento

CHUMASH (CHOO-mash)—Native American tribe in southern California

CHURN—wooden bucket with a paddle used to make butter from milk

CONESTOGA WAGON—large wagon used on East Coast, not suitable for travel west

HALTER LOOP—type of knot used to lead animals without choking them

HUNTER GATHERERS—people who hunt animals and gather wild plants to live

MIWOK—Native American people in central California

MORSE, Samuel F. B.—created a receiver and code for messages using telegraphs

OLIVELLA (ol-ih-VEL-a)—shell used by Chumash people as money

PIÑATA (peen-YA-ta)—papier mâché toy filled with treats and broken open at parties

PRAIRIE SCHOONER—small wagon used by most pioneers heading west

SHINNY—game of ball played by Native American peoples

SQUARE KNOT—most common form of binding knot to tie parcels

TELEGRAPH—machine that uses electric pulses to send messages

TIMBER HITCH—type of knot used to drag logs

TORTILLAS (tor-TEE-yas)—flat fried bread

TRANSCONTINENTAL RAILROAD—railroad line uniting western and eastern United States

UNION PACIFIC RAILROAD—built transcontinental railroad west from Omaha, Nebraska

YOKE—set of two animals side by side joined by a harness

Bibliography

Barchers, Suzanne I., and Patricia C. Marden. *Cooking up U.S. History*: Recipes and Research to Shape with Children, 2nd Ed., Englewood, CO: Teacher Ideas Press, 1999.

Caduto, Michael J., and Joseph Bruchac. *Keepers of the Earth*. Golden, CO: Fulcrum, Inc., 1997.

Carlson, Laurie. *Westward Ho!* Chicago: Chicago Review Press, 1996.

Culin, Stewart. *Games of the North American Indians. Volume 1—Games of Chance*. Lincoln, NE: University of Nebraska Press, 1992.

Culin, Stewart. *Games of the North American Indians. Volume 2—Games of Skill*. Lincoln, NE: University of Nebraska Press, 1992.

Day, Nancy. *Your Travel Guide to Ancient Mayan Civilization*. Minneapolis, MN: Runestone Press, 2001.

Dineen, Jacqueline. *Worlds of the Past: The Romans*. New York: New Discovery Books, 1992.

Eaton, Herbert. *The Overland Trail to California in 1852*. New York: GP Putnam's Sons, 1974.

Galvin, Irene Flum. *Cultures of the Past: The Ancient Maya*. New York: Benchmark Books, 1997.

Hakim, Joy. *Making Thirteen Colonies*. New York: Oxford University Press, 1993.

Heizer, Robert F., Volume Ed. *Handbook of North American Indians Vol. 8*. Washington, DC: Smithsonian Institution, 1978.

Hewitt, James, Ed. *Eye-Witnesses to Wagon Trains West*. New York: Charles Scribner's Sons, 1973.

Hinds, Kathyrn. *Cultures of the Past: The Ancient Romans*. New York: Benchmark Books, 1997.

Hofmann, Charles. *American Indians Sing*. New York: The John Day Company, 1967.

Hofsinde, Robert (Gray-Wolf). *Indians on the Move*. New York: William Morrow & Company, 1970.

King, David C. *Pioneer Days*. New York: John Wiley & Sons, Inc., 1997.

Malam, John. *Exploring Ancient Greece*. London: Evans Brothers Ltd., 1999.

Marston, Elsa. *Cultures of the Past—The Ancient Egyptians*. New York: Benchmark Books, 1996.

The Mayans Illustrated Historical Profile. Cancun, Mexico: Universal Image Enterprise, Inc., 1993.

Milliken, Linda. *China—Exploring a Culture through Arts, Crafts, Cooking, Games, and Historical Aids*. Dana Point, CA: Edupress, 1995.

Roberts, J. M. *The Illustrated History of the World, Volumes 1, 2, and 3*. New York: Oxford University Press, 1999.

Sakurai, Gail. *The Thirteen Colonies*. New York: Children's Press, 2000.

Sheehan, Sean, and Pat Levy. *The Ancient World—Rome*. Austin, TX: Raintree Steck-Vaugh, 1999.

Shuter, Jane. *The Ancient World: Egypt*. Austin, TX: Raintree Steck-Vaughn, 1999.

Steins, Richard. *The Making of America: Colonial America*. Austin, TX: Raintree Steck-Vaugh, 2000.

Thomas, David Hurst. *Exploring Native North America*. New York: Oxford University Press, 2000.

World Book Encyclopedia. Chicago: World Book, Inc., 2000.

Index

About the Author

Author and illustrator Carol Peterson holds a degree in International Relations from the University of California. Her unique hands-on approach to teaching stems from her studies of history, geography, sociology, economics, and political science, combined with her devotion to instilling in kids the joy of learning.

Over the past ten years, thousands of children have enjoyed the many educational activities Carol has developed for schools, scouting groups, and children's charities. Carol lives in California with her husband and two teenage children.